P9-AQX-533

The Seven Queens of England

The Seven Queens of England

GEOFFREY TREASE

Author of "Web of Traitors," "Sir Walter Raleigh," "Cue For Treason," etc.

THE VANGUARD PRESS, INC.
NEW YORK

Library of Congress Card Catalogue Number: 53–6900

Manufactured in the United States of America by H. Wolff Book Manufacturing Company, New York, N. Y.
Designed by Marshall Lee

Seventh Printing

CONTENTS

The Seven Queens of England

A TAPESTRY OF QUEENS

Today, for the seventh time in history, a queen rules England in her own right. She is a sovereign, not merely the consort of a husband reigning as king.

"Seventh" requires a word of explanation. Maud, otherwise known as Matilda, is often omitted from the list of English monarchs, but there seems no logical reason for this. Her legal right was much stronger than that of her rival Stephen, and her effective control of the country was as great—and as small—as his. True, she was never crowned at Westminster, but that does not make her any less a sovereign. Edward VIII was a king throughout 1936, though he abdicated before his coronation and became the Duke of Windsor. The roll of these queens must, therefore, open with Maud, in the far-off mists of the twelfth century.

This is not meant to be a history book, covering seven periods. It is offered rather as a miniature portrait gallery of the seven queens, with their personal stories attached. If more space has sometimes been given to their girlhood than to their old age, there is a good reason: those early years are likely to be of more interest to general readers, though not perhaps to political historians.

A tapestry would be an even better comparison than a portrait gallery. For in the unrolling of a long tapestry one can sometimes trace a recurring pattern—and in reading the actual happenings of long ago, what is more fascinating than the tracing of similar patterns and their variations?

Two constant threads run, inevitably, through the story of each queen. The question, Shall I ever reach the throne? and the later question, Whom shall I marry? The questions make the pattern, and the answers provide the variations.

A boy can be *born* to be King of England. No girl ever can be "born to be Queen." A surprising number of English kings have not been the eldest sons of their predecessors, but at least any king's eldest son knows for certain that, unless he dies before his father, he will inherit the throne. No princess can ever be sure of that so long as there is any chance of a younger brother being born—or even a half brother, if her father should marry again. There is thus an element of special uncertainty in the early life of each future queen which adds a drama of its own.

No less drama is involved in the second question. It matters a good deal whom a king marries and raises to the throne beside him, but a queen's choice of partner matters infinitely more, especially in periods when a sovereign wields vast personal power. The question occurs in each of these life stories, but it is answered in various ways. One queen may marry an illustrious nobody, one may be dominated by a greater personality than her own, and yet another may deliberately choose not to share her power.

That last choice brings in another question; Who will rule after me? Only one queen made the decision not to marry at all, but a remarkable number of the others had no children to succeed them, so that this third question provides us with a third thread running through most of our tapestry. Doubt as to the succession, with all that it implies in terms of plots, invasions, and revolutions, brings further drama to the tale of the English queens.

A fourth strand in the pattern is the somber one of religious conflict. It plays a vital part in four of these seven lives, since four of the queens happened to live in times when faith, whether Catholic or Protestant, was the chief political issue dividing both England and Europe alike. Even to this day it is laid down by Parliament that the sovereign must be a Protestant and take a coronation oath accordingly; but her subjects have enjoyed complete religious freedom for so long that passions are no longer stirred by this or by other historical reminders, and there is no difference in loyalty or affection among the Catholics, Protestants, and others over whom she rules. It is impossible to write of the sixteenth and seventeenth centuries without stirring tragic memories of religious strife: one can only do one's best to record events fairly and, at the same time, indicate how they affected people of both sides who were caught up in them and could not see as clearly as can the modern historian with all the facts before him. One tries to hold the balance evenly, and hopes that no present-day reader will see offense to his own faith where none is intended.

The fifth strand in the pattern may be thought of as golden rather than black. There is a common idea that England is always most prosperous when ruled by a woman. How far is this backed by history? After reading the first six of these life stories, the reader may well agree that most of the later queens have brought, if not peace and plenty, at least power and plenty. As for the future, the famous English poet, Cecil Day Lewis, has already warned his countrymen to rely rather on their own efforts than on a memory of the past. "An age is as young as it feels," he says, "and unless we are quite sure that we feel as young, as vigorous, and as hopeful as the England of the sixteenth century, we had better not start calling ourselves the new Elizabethans. Otherwise we shall be merely acting a part, and a part for which we are not suited."

Such then is the pattern of our tapestry. One word more before it is unrolled for detailed examination. Where are we, in history, when the weaving of it began?

The present Queen of England traces her ancestry back to the Saxon kings, before Alfred the Great. That is well over a thousand years and there is nothing doubtful or mythical about the record. But our present chronicle need not stretch back so far. The first woman to claim the throne of England was Maud, the granddaughter of William the Conqueror. Our story opens at the beginning of the twelfth century, when Saxon England was still slowly and reluctantly absorbing Norman ways, and when there were men, still only middle-aged, who could remember the charging knights and rattling arrows of the Battle of Hastings.

♁

MAUD, MOTHER OF THE PLANTAGENETS

Such a thing had never been known before.

Under the high rafters of the hall, the long-robed barons murmured doubtfully together. Bishops and abbots moved among them, smooth faces masking the thoughts which raced inside their tonsured skulls.

Henry I was not a king to be crossed lightly, even by the combined power of lords and churchmen met together in his Great Council. He had made his wishes known, and not for nothing was he William the Conqueror's son.

If he were to die without leaving a son of his own to succeed him, they must at once proclaim his daughter, Maud, sovereign lady of the English. For that purpose they were called together today, to swear a solemn oath.

But who, muttered some of the Council, had ever heard of such a thing? When, either in England or in Normandy, had a woman ever reigned? Once, in the misty Saxon past, four or five centuries before, it was said that a Saxon queen had ruled for a single year—but this was the harsh, real world of 1126. It was only sixty years since the Conqueror had brought off his colossal gamble at the Battle of Hastings. England still needed the iron fingers of a man to mold it into Norman shape. At home and on the Continent it was an age of wars, revolts, and the unceasing blackmail of threatened force. It was no time for the fantastic experiment of a woman ruler.

Nobody ventured to argue the matter with the King.

Henry stood there, a still handsome man in his late fifties, though the tragic loss of his only son, some years before, had drawn deep lines in his face and silvered the once dark curly hair and the trim beard. He had not the height of his famous father, but he was powerfully built, and his voice held an echo of that ringing tone which had once rallied the wavering Norman ranks at Hastings. When he called on the members of the Great Council to come forward one by one and take the oath of allegiance to Maud, there was no holding back.

First came the churchmen: the archbishops, bishops, abbots. . . . Next, King David of Scotland, doing homage for the estates he held in England. . . . Then, leading the earls and barons of England and Normandy, Henry's nephew, Stephen of Blois, the handsomest knight in Christendom. . . .

It was an electric moment, as Stephen took the oath to his cousin. He, too, was the Conqueror's grandchild, through his mother, and he was well aware that many would have preferred him as heir to the throne, though his claim was weaker in law.

Maud was as beautiful as Stephen was handsome, with, what is more, a dignity of bearing he never had. From childhood she had been an empress and the foremost lady in Europe, though now, at twenty-three, she was back at her father's court as a widow.

It is recorded that she was much impressed by her dashing young cousin. It was unlucky that they were too closely related and that, in any case, he had just married someone else. For a marriage between Maud and Stephen, had it only been possible, would have saved all dispute over the throne and spared England the agony of those long years of civil war, when it seemed (as the chronicler wrote) "as though Christ and his Saints were asleep."

To understand the drama of Maud and Stephen we must be able to picture the stage on which it was enacted.

She was born in London in the late autumn of 1102. Most of us, who do not know a great deal of history, have a vague, general picture in our minds which we label "the Middle Ages." It probably includes Robin Hood, the Canterbury Pilgrims, castles, cathedrals, and coats-of-arms. It is of little use in helping us to imagine Maud's background, for Robin Hood came long after her time and neither Friar Tuck nor any other friar set foot in England until the next century. The six-foot bow had yet to be introduced; so had the lovely science of heraldry.

Thomas à Becket was scarcely born, let alone martyred, so there could be no pilgrims to his shrine and no Chaucer to report them. Canterbury Cathedral itself was there, but very different from what a visitor sees today; and the same must be said of nearly all the other ancient churches and castles which delight the modern tourist. That delicate tracery, those pointed arches, flying buttresses, and richly decorated screens still belonged—together with lofty curtain walls, circular bastions, and most of the other features we associate with castle ruins—to a future unimagined by the people of Maud's day.

Twelfth-century England was a densely forested country, thinly populated with about two million people. Of these, a fair number must already have been living in London, which had been an important place throughout England's early history. We have an interesting description of the city by Fitzstephen and, though he must have been wildly exaggerating when he wrote that London mustered twenty thousand cavalry and sixty thousand infantry to fight against Maud, he was presumably telling the truth when he said that there were fifty churches. Even in "the age of Faith," when churchgoing was universal, that figure suggests a considerable population.

The other towns (about ninety in number) could only have been very small, scarcely more than large villages by our modern reckoning. Two or three thousand inhabitants were enough to put a place high in the list of famous cities. Usually the steep-roofed houses huddled close together under the lee of some protecting fortress or monastery, with perhaps a ditch and stockade of their own, being replaced about this date by a stone wall.

For the rest, England was a land of villages, each with its broad belt of commons, meadows, and land plowed in long strips. Woodland, swamp, and hunting forests (the last, often semi-open riding country, like the African bush) filled the wilder tracts between. This forest was still extending rather than diminishing—in Hampshire alone the Conqueror had turned out five hundred families from thirty-two villages, to add twenty thousand acres to his hunting ground. Untamed rivers—unbanked, undredged, with few of the bridges and none of the locks we can see today—alternately raced and dawdled to the sea as the rainfall varied. Even so, they formed the best means of transport for heavy goods. No one had built a road in England since the Romans. Messengers, travelers, and armies moved as best they could along the fading, grass-grown ways.

This was the England Maud's grandfather had conquered thirty or forty years before. This was the England her father, his barons, and his bishops were slowly shaping to the Norman pattern, putting stone churches in place of wooden, and raising massive square strongholds where earthen mounds and timber stockades had stood before. This was the England that someday, perhaps, she must try to rule.

Maud's mother, Matilda, was the King of Scotland's daughter but descended also from the Saxon kings of England. It is through her that the present Queen claims descent from Alfred the Great. Matilda* had been strictly brought up by her Aunt Christina, the abbess of a convent in the south of England. It is probable that, as a very small girl, Maud was educated at the same royal abbey of Wilton and very much in the same tradition of the Saxon nobility. For girls that meant a thorough grounding in housekeeping, not merely in ornamental needlework but in spinning, weaving, dressmaking, poultry keeping, and dairying. Most of the queen's ladies were chosen from the old Saxon aristocracy, so that Maud's childhood was thoroughly English, except for her religious training, which fell to the great Italian, Anselm, then Archbishop of Canterbury. But even he was a friend of her mother's, who attracted to herself all the outstanding personalities of her time, whether scholars, artists, or musicians.

The first seven years of a child's life are said to be the most vital to its character. At any rate, they were all that the poor little Princess was fated to enjoy of her mother's cultured society, the saintly archbishop's moral guidance, and the company of her brother William. For in 1109 she had to say good-bye to all of them.

In that year, at Whitsuntide, there arrived in London a magnificent embassy from the Emperor Henry V, ruler of the Holy Roman Empire. The

* Maud herself was often known as Matilda. To avoid confusion, Matilda is here used to refer to her mother, and Maud for the future empress—especially since Stephen's wife was yet another Matilda.

German ambassadors (for Germany was the central core of that empire) were "remarkable for their great stature and splendid attire." They had come to ask for Maud's hand in marriage to their imperial master.

What did the girl think of it, with her seventh birthday still to come? We can only guess.

She was old enough to know, at least, that in spite of all the old romances, highborn girls seldom married for love, and that a king's daughter, espepecially, must take the husband arranged for her. Princesses were made to be used, like sealing wax, for the making of treaties and alliances.

Had she possessed such a thing as an atlas, she could have seen that the Holy Roman Empire was a vast area, covering roughly what is now Germany, Austria, Czechoslovakia, Holland, Belgium, Switzerland, Corsica, Sardinia, and Italy as far south as Rome, together with the dependent kingdoms of Denmark, Poland, and Hungary. Even without an accurate map, she knew that her future husband was the most powerful ruler in the world. And, had she paused to wonder why so mighty an emperor should wish to marry her, any of the courtiers could have supplied the answer. Her father was the strongest king outside the Empire—his barons well under control and his position with the Pope satisfactory—and there was no man whose friendship would be more useful to the German Henry.

So it was all arranged. Maud set off for Dover with an escort of lords and ladies, crossed to Boulogne, and, riding on to Liege, saw her future husband for the first time. He was then twenty-eight, she was just seven. She saw that he was fairly good-looking. She marked too the profound respect with which his courtiers treated him—these Germans were stiffer, more ceremonious, less free-and-easy than the English. It must have been more like meeting a new uncle. Certainly there was no romance in the encounter. If Maud was ever truly in love during her life (which has been doubted), it was not with the Emperor.

Henry was not looking for love. He wanted an alliance with England and, in due time, a satisfactory partner for the imperial throne—a woman who, though not German by birth, should be as German as he could make her.

To that end he packed off her retinue back to England and handed her over to the care of Bruno, archbishop of Trier. She was to be taught the German language and the German ways. Letters from England must have been few, slow, and uncertain. Every other link with her parents and her former life was broken. Far away, amid the vine-clad hills of the Holy Roman Empire, the small English girl stiffened into a German princess.

Maud was a success in Germany, more popular perhaps with the imperial nobility than she ever was to be with the barons of England. Apart from her natural good looks, she had a dignity of bearing which, with the years, developed into the majesty that was expected of her.

When she had been, as it were, on approval for

some time, the betrothal was formally celebrated and she was crowned Queen of the Romans in Mainz Cathedral. Medieval girls came of age at twelve, so in 1114 the actual wedding took place, in that same cathedral, and her coronation was solemnly repeated. It was a glorious affair, attended by all the chivalry of Christendom. Five archbishops and thirty bishops were present. The Duke of Bohemia acted as cupbearer to the bridegroom. Other dukes, with innumerable counts and barons, made a shimmering sea of cloth of gold. There were wedding gifts of incomparable splendor.

Maud's dowry from England, raised by heavy taxation which was provided for under the feudal system on the marriage of a king's eldest daughter, amounted to £824,000. It can hardly have made her more popular in the land where few had ever seen her, and even fewer expected ever to do so again.

Time passed. Maud matured into a beautiful girl, though her life did not leave much scope for girlishness. Dignity was laid on her shoulders too early. She was inclined to be cold and reserved. How could she be otherwise, married to a man old enough to be her father, and raised so high above everyone else that ordinary friendships and affections were impossible? She kept her bargain—the Emperor had England's friendship and a dignified empress to share his throne—but no children were born to humanize the marriage.

When she was fifteen she joined the Emperor in Italy, where he had marched with his army in an attempt to impose his will upon the Pope. The latter fled from Rome rather than agree to crown Henry Holy Roman Emperor, so a French archbishop was persuaded to do so instead, and was excommunicated immediately afterward. Maud shared in this doubtful ceremony, and heard the soldiers cheering and hailing her as Empress of the Romans.

While in Rome, she had a welcome visitor, Ralph d'Escures, who had succeeded her childhood tutor, Anselm, as Archbishop of Canterbury. He was probably the most important English visitor she had received since leaving home, and it must have been good to talk at leisure with someone who was in close contact with her parents. He must have been one of the last, also, to bring firsthand news of her mother, for on the first of May in the following year, while the unwitting people of England were busy with their traditional springtime revels, "the Good Queen"—as she was deservedly called—died and was soon afterward laid to rest in Westminster Abbey. Four years later Maud was to hear that she had a stepmother, Adelicia of Louvain, known as "the fair maid of Brabant" and no older than herself. It says something for both their characters that Maud and Adelicia eventually became lifelong friends.

Meanwhile, Maud saw no future for herself outside the Empire.

She must have made good use of her early training and shown Henry that she was old enough to take responsibility, for, when he had to leave Italy, she remained as his official deputy. Round about her sixteenth birthday she was presiding over a council at Castrocaro, between the Apennines and the Adriatic Sea. The next year she returned to Germany to join him.

A year later came tragic news from home.

Her only brother, William, had been drowned in the wreck of the *White Ship,* crossing the Channel from Normandy. There had been a wild party on board, the crew had joined in the drinking, and the vessel had struck a rock. Though William had got safely into a boat, he had gone back to rescue some of the others, but they had crowded in pell-mell, and the boat had capsized. A little earlier in the voyage Stephen of Blois, not liking the look of things, had quietly transferred himself to another ship.

Maud was now well-versed in statecraft. Even as she mourned her brother, she could not help being aware, also, that the tragedy might have far-reaching effects. But she could not then, in 1120, foresee how deeply she herself would be concerned.

Less than five years later, the Emperor himself was dead, at the comparatively early age of forty-four. Maud was a childless widow. Someone else's son would be chosen to rule the Empire, but she had made herself so popular that she was pressed to remain in Germany and choose a second husband among the unmarried princes.

Maud refused. Her prospects had altered. Her stepmother was childless too, and her father was begging her to come home. It could only be a matter of time before the English crown would come to her.

She went home, and all the nobility of England, Stephen included, swore to accept her as their future queen.

Young widows, in those days, could do one of two things: marry again or become nuns. Only seldom were they able to keep their independence.

Maud obviously could not disappear into a convent, so, very soon, King Henry arranged for her to marry Geoffrey Plantagenet, whose father was Count of Anjou, a small area of France bordering Brittany. This time, the bridegroom was ten years younger than the bride. Geoffrey was barely sixteen. He was a good-looking boy, nicknamed "the Handsome," but inclined to be self-willed and conceited. This conceit was made worse a year later when his father went off to seek his fortune in Palestine (where he remained as King of Jerusalem) and the boy found himself Count of Anjou.

It was not likely that a strong-minded young woman like Maud, who had worn the crown of an empress, was going to submit meekly to a boy-husband, and the marriage was rather a stormy affair, with quarrels and separations. But these were patched up, and in 1133 a son was born to them at Le Mans who was destined to become Henry II, one of England's strongest kings, and to establish the royal line of the Plantagenets. Maud shed tears of happiness at his christening. It was the only time in her life, say the historians, that she was seen to weep.

Other children followed quickly: Geoffrey in

1134 and William in 1136. Unfortunately, these otherwise happy events could hardly have come at a worse time from the political point of view. King Henry died suddenly on December 1, 1135. Maud should have ridden posthaste to Normandy, crossed to England by the swiftest ship available, and had herself proclaimed Queen of England. Her babies and her own health (she had been seriously ill the previous year) made this impossible.

Stephen of Blois saw his chance and took it. He hurried to London, where he was popular with the citizens, and thence to Winchester, the old capital, where he seized the royal treasure and the late King's crown. Two days before Christmas, that crown was placed on his head in Westminster Abbey, and his supporters were hailing him as King.

It was a long time before Maud could counter these rapid moves. Her hands were tied. She appealed to the Pope: the result was vague, but unfavorable to her as far as it went. Her uncle, King David of Scotland, invaded the North of England to support her claim. He was bought off the first time, and, on his second appearance, crushingly defeated at the Battle of the Standards, at Northallerton, by Stephen's supporter, the fighting Archbishop of York. In Normandy—the other part of the disputed inheritance—Stephen fought a campaign against Maud's husband. The only effect of this was to make both the rivals equally unpopular with the people they claimed as subjects. It was not until nearly four years after King Henry's death, when

Stephen had squandered most of the royal treasure, quarreled with his leading supporters in the Church and the government, and reduced his own affairs to confusion, that Maud's long-delayed opportunity arrived. Inspired by her half brother, Robert, Earl of Gloucester, the West of England flared into revolt against the usurper, and in October, 1139, Maud herself landed at Portsmouth with a small force of a hundred and forty knights.

For some reason, hard to understand now, she did not make straight for the West Country where her support lay. Instead, she rode to the great castle of Arundel, in Sussex, where her stepmother (now herself remarried) gave her a friendly welcome. This visit was nearly fatal to Maud's chances. Suddenly Stephen, who had been besieging Corfe Castle in Dorset, appeared with his army beneath the walls of Arundel.

Arundel Castle might well have withstood a siege. But would the garrison, apart from Maud's own knights, resist? Adelicia's new husband, d'Albini, had no wish to quarrel with Stephen. The outlook for Maud was black. Stephen could have made her prisoner and either held her or deported her across the Channel, where, he considered, she belonged.

Stephen's easygoing character saved her. He was a kindly man, generous and chivalrous, but he had no foresight, no intellectual grasp, no ability to distinguish good advice from bad. In this present situation it was against his knightly instincts to make war on women; and at the same time (in contradiction of these instincts) he listened to the foolish argument that, if he left Maud free to gather her supporters in the West, he would be better able to smash them at a single blow.

So Maud rode forth from Arundel with all honor, with Stephen's safe-conduct and his own brother to escort her, and went to Bristol, the chief stronghold of her party.

There is no point in chronicling the detailed ebb and flow of the long civil war which devastated England for the next few years. Neither claimant could win over a really overwhelming majority of supporters. Stephen was liked, but he did not inspire people. He excelled in personal contacts and was, if anything, too familiar. He was fairly described as "no king, only the first and best of the barons." Maud, on the other hand, offended Englishmen by being too cold and distant, in the German manner which had been forced upon her as a child. With this was joined the hardness and pride of her Norman ancestry and the traditional obstinacy of the Saxon. She had the courage and enterprise of a man. Perhaps if her more feminine qualities had not been so thwarted when she was young, she might have won more support in England.

However, she made a good beginning.

Setting up her capital in Bristol, she quickly restored order in the territory she controlled. This was a period when local barons—seeing the breakdown of national government—became a law to themselves and turned their castles into robber-strongholds. As the *Anglo-Saxon Chronicle* records in a famous passage:

> "When the castles were made they filled them with devils and evil men. Then they took those men whom they deemed to have any possessions, husbandmen and women, and put them in prison for gold and silver and tortured them with unspeakable torture. They put them in dungeons in which there were adders and snakes and toads. . . . They robbed and burned all the towns, so thou mightest well go all a day's journey and thou wouldest never find a man settled in a town, nor the land tilled. . . ."

But at least the area directly controlled by Maud was well governed.

In the course of the next year or two, support for her spread through other parts of the country. Two of her followers seized Lincoln Castle by a trick. Stephen marched to Lincoln, and was there met by Maud's growing army, under the Earl of Gloucester. This included a strong force of Welsh infantry and a body of picked shock troops, known as "the Disinherited" because they had all lost their lands by supporting Maud and had everything to gain by her victory.

Stephen's chief supporters ran away. Stephen, who was certainly no coward, was left dismounted, defending himself with a Danish battle-ax he had snatched up. Seeing matters were hopeless, he surrendered. Maud hurried to Winchester, received the crown, and proclaimed herself Queen.

At this critical moment, Maud's pride was her undoing. Her rival was safely imprisoned in her own stronghold at Bristol, but his very able wife had still an unbeaten army in Kent. London, as always, favored Stephen. There were countless people to be handled tactfully and won over to her side—churchmen and barons and the citizens of her capital—before Maud could be formally crowned at Westminster.

She never was. For some mysterious reason which can never now be understood—unless it was the state of her health at the time, affecting her moods and behavior, and the natural reaction after so many years of waiting—Maud's common sense seemed to desert her during those few vital months. She had shown herself a wise and patient woman before; she was a wise and patient woman afterward; but just then, on the eve of her coronation, she managed to offend all the people whose help she most needed.

Worst of all, she talked to the free and independent Londoners as though she were still the Holy Roman Empress. Their answer was revolt. As she sat down to dinner in the Palace of Westminster on Midsummer Day, feeling perfectly secure, she was astounded to learn that London had risen and that Stephen's wife was leading an army through the gates.

There was just time to mount a horse and escape. Maud and her party rode hell-for-leather to Oxford, sixty miles away. She held one ace in her hand: Stephen himself, still captive at Bristol. Otherwise, the civil war must be fought and won again.

It was fought, but it was never won. Maud led her army with the courage and energy of her grandfather, William the Conqueror. She surprised the old castle at Winchester, laid siege to the new one, and was herself besieged. When supplies ran short, she resolved to make a dash for it. She rode out early one morning, to be followed later by her half brother. As the country was alive with enemy troops, the two parties went by different routes. The Earl was the unlucky one: he was attacked as he was crossing the little Hampshire river, Test, and taken prisoner. Pausing at Ludgershall for him to overtake her, Maud realized that something had gone wrong and that she herself was in mortal danger. She remounted and galloped for Devizes, thirty miles away. She arrived there exhausted, unable to keep in the saddle any longer. But it would have been folly to rest, with Stephen's followers scouring the countryside for her, and her iron will forced her on. She had herself strapped in a litter between two horses and carried to Gloucester with all speed. There, in her loyal West Country, she would be safe.

It was not the last of her dramatic escapes. The capture of her half brother forced her, after some hard bargaining, to release Stephen in exchange. In the autumn of 1142, Stephen besieged her in Oxford Castle, and this resulted in the most famous episode of her life.

Again the garrison's supplies were running short, and again Maud decided to make a dash for it, knowing that the main object of the siege was to capture her. Even the gentlemanly Stephen had got over his reluctance to make war on a lady, if that lady was his cousin Maud.

This time conditions were very different. Christmas was near, and the weather was unusually bitter. Not only was the foggy Thames valley deep in snow, but the river itself was covered with thick ice, which seldom happens more than once in ten or twenty winters.

Dressed all in white, with three knights similarly camouflaged, Maud was let down by ropes from the ramparts. Stephen's men held the town to the east of the fortress, but the way was clear to the riverbank. The four ghostly figures passed noiselessly and unchallenged through the silvery gloom. The ice held. The Thames wound dimly in front of them between its low hills, offering them a highway to safety. The snow formed a thick carpet even over the ice, but at least the going was easier than through the deep drifts on land. Seven or eight miles of hard trudging through the night brought them to the great abbey of Abingdon, where they got horses to continue their journey to Wallingford.

So, with sieges and escapes, marchings and countermarchings, the civil war went on its weary way. England was in a state of anarchy. Maud controlled some areas and Stephen others, but whole regions took little notice of either. Lords changed sides as suited them, and might was right. Neither of the royal rivals could ever muster sufficient strength to crush the other.

As Maud never recaptured London, her coronation at Westminster never took place, but this fact cannot, by itself, weaken her claim to be the lawful sovereign during those years. Sometimes she styled herself *Anglorum regina,* "Queen of the English," but more often, *Anglorum domina,* "Lady of the English." But whatever form of words she used, she left no doubt in anyone's mind that she considered herself the rightful ruler of both England and Normandy, where her husband kept up a warfare parallel with her own against Stephen's Norman supporters. Maud's early training by the German archbishop had given her a clear vision of political power. She always knew that the real thing was something much more than words and titles.

She showed this when, in 1153, the two sides had fought themselves to a standstill. Her faithful half brother had died of fever and her other chief allies were dead. Stephen, on the other hand, had lost his son and heir, and it may be that Maud guessed that her rival himself had not long to live. At all events, she agreed to make peace by the Treaty of Wallingford. She resigned the crown to Stephen while he lived. On his death, it was to come to her eldest son, Henry, now a forceful young knight of twenty.

So it came about. Stephen died in the following year, and on the nineteenth of December, in Westminister Abbey, the crown was placed upon the close-cropped, reddish head of Henry II, first of the Plantagenet kings who were to rule England until the end of the Middle Ages. Maud had no reason to feel that her long struggle had been in vain. In giving up the crown for a little while, she had made it safe for her son and her son's sons.

Nor, though she now withdrew into the background, did she relax her energies. She was a help to Henry throughout the first ten years of his reign, and undoubtedly it was her wisdom and experience which saved him from worse mistakes than he did make and enabled him to become one of the greatest medieval kings. He, passionate and strong-willed though he was, listened to his mother when he would listen to no one else. The martyr Becket might never have been murdered had Maud lived longer.

She died in 1167, at Rouen, in Normandy. In her last years, as befitted an elderly lady in those days, she busied herself with good works. She had always been generous to churches and monasteries; now she was even more active, building and endowing. She gave Rouen a magnificent new stone bridge, crossing the Seine by thirteen arches. But such charities were not enough to absorb the tireless energies of one who had been both queen and empress, and she spent her last months, bedridden and feeble though she was, collecting military intelligence in the war against King Louis of France. Her chief agent was the Prior of St. Barbara's, near Lisieux, who collected information about French troop movements from a network of his own spies, and passed it to Maud for transmission to her son. The regular go-between was a monk, and the actual papers were hidden in his luxuriant beard.

So Maud died, a fighter to the end, and was

buried as she had always meant to be, in the abbey church of Bec, in Normandy. Nearly four centuries passed before another woman tried to govern England.

THE YEARS BETWEEN

1167–1516

The Plantagenet family ruled England until the end of the Middle Ages—first, Maud's ruthless but efficient son, Henry II, then her grandsons, Richard I (Lionheart) and John (who granted Magna Charta to his rebellious barons), and later her descendants, including such kings as Henry V, the victor of Agincourt. England grew powerful, absorbed Wales, seized part of Ireland, but failed to conquer Scotland. For a long time the Plantagenets held great tracts of French territory, until Joan of Arc roused her countrymen against them. By the end of this period, England's foothold in Europe had shrunk to the port of Calais, the loss of which was to be such a grief to Mary I. Apart from wars, this age saw the flowering of medieval civilization in the sublime architecture of cathedrals and the exquisite craftsmanship of sculptor and wood carver. It produced Geoffrey Chaucer, the poet;

John Wycliffe, the translator of the Bible; William Caxton, the printer; and many other great men whose names are still honored.

In the fifteenth century came the bitter strife between two rival branches of the royal family, now called the Wars of the Roses. In the Battle of Bosworth (1485), the last Plantagenet, Richard III, was killed. His conqueror, Henry Tudor, had a poor claim to the throne but strengthened it by marriage. With him, Henry VII, we leave behind the Middle Ages and enter the Tudor period. He was succeeded in 1509 by his son, Henry VIII, whose reign saw the Reformation and the plunging of England into tragic conflicts of religion. Henry VIII was the father of the next two queens, Mary I and Elizabeth I.

ꝏ

MARY, QUITE CONTRARY...

There is an old English nursery rhyme which begins:

> *"Mary, Mary, quite contrary,*
> *How does your garden grow?"*

But of all the people who know those words, how many could say who "Mary" was? How many realize that this apparently harmless jingle, chanted by generations of small children and their mothers, probably began as a dangerous political gesture—a mocking cry of defiance from the persecuted underground of Tudor England? "Quite contrary" . . . How perfectly the two words sum up Mary I, as she seemed to her enemies!

She was born February 18, 1516, at Greenwich Palace, overlooking one of the last silvery loops of the Thames as it glides seaward below London. Her father, Henry VIII, was still the Prince Charming of Europe. Barely twenty-five, six feet two in height, both an athlete and a man of culture, he was thus described by one who knew him: "His Majesty is the handsomest potentate I ever set eyes on. He speaks French, English, Latin, and a little Italian; plays well on the lute and harpsichord, sings from the book at sight, draws the bow with greater strength than any man in England, and jousts marvelously. . . . He is very fond of hunting. . . . He is extremely fond of tennis, at which game it is the prettiest thing in the world to see him play, his fair skin glowing through a shirt of the finest texture. . . . He is very religious and hears three Masses daily when he hunts, and sometimes five on other days."

Mary's mother was the noble and virtuous Catherine of Aragon. Her portrait, painted about a year before, shows her in one of those angular head-dresses still worn by queens on our playing cards. Indeed, perhaps we may think of Catherine as rather *like* a playing-card queen—beautiful, a trifle stiff, a card of value in the game but one which can always, if necessary, be beaten by the king.

For godfather the royal baby had the other foremost figure of the day: Cardinal Wolsey, who, men whispered, ruled England in Henry's name and had dreams of a crown himself—the papal crown of Rome.

With such parents and such a godfather, what girl could have looked forward more confidently to the future? And for the first few years, as the King proudly displayed her to courtiers and ambassadors, boasting, *"Ista puella nunquam plorat!"* (This girl never cries!), Mary had little cause for tears. Sorrow came later—from the brother who was never born.

It was four hundred years from Maud to Mary; it is another four hundred years from Mary to ourselves. Life has changed more rapidly and more noticeably in the second of these two periods, but, even so, the England of the Tudors was very different from that of the Plantagenets.

The population had doubled itself to nearly four millions. Henry could still hunt at will in the greenwood, but the wastelands had shrunk, especially in the North, where the Cistercian monks had long since tamed the wild valleys into sheep farms. Towns were bigger, there were more bridges, and the roads were safer, though they were not much better. The hovels of the people were giving place to the brick or stone cottages, with their crisscross patterning of oaken beams, their pointed gables and small-paned windows, which can still be seen at Stratford-upon-Avon and a hundred other places in England today.

Above all, the barons and their castles—both so important in Maud's story—had lost much of their power. Many of the old nobility had been wiped out in the Wars of the Roses, which Mary's grandfather, Henry VII, had ended with his victory at Bosworth, thirty years before. There were still lords in England, for Henry had filled the empty ranks with new men he could trust; but he did not trust them far enough to give them any chance to dispute his power again. As for their castles, the new artillery could deal with them, and only the King had the cannons. Great gentlemen might go on living in their castles, but they built no new ones. This was to be the century of the first country mansions —vast places with forests of tall and twisting chimneys, thousands of flashing windows, and rooms for every day in the year. A palace, not a fortress, was the new ideal.

In such mansions, and in the much smaller manor houses which were to be found in almost every village, Mary spent most of her life.

A royal child can seldom expect to see as much of her parents as other children do. Mary usually spent Christmas and Easter with the King and Queen; she might be brought to Greenwich Palace for some other special occasion, or she might see her parents when they went "on progress," that is, on tour, through the countryside; but most of her early years were passed at Ditton Park or Hanworth, both near London, in the care of the Countess of Salisbury and Lady Margaret Bryan.

She was a good-looking little girl, with a clear skin and the reddish hair of the Tudors. Sorrow and fear had not yet tightened her lips or brought the shadows to her eyes. Yet, at an age when modern children are scarcely being bothered with the alphabet, she was struggling with the heavy education which the sixteenth century imposed on girls as well as boys, if they were of noble birth.

French, Spanish, Italian, Latin . . . what sort of children *were* these Tudors, that they could keep four or five different languages separate in their small heads, at the age of six or seven? Perhaps they did not remember very much—though their letters and speeches in later life suggest that they did—but that they remembered anything at all must seem to us rather wonderful.

She was taught Latin by the King's doctor, the great scholar Linacre, who wrote a grammar specially for her. Her Latin exercises were corrected by the Queen. It was the Queen, too, when Mary was seven, who asked the Spanish scholar, Vives, to draw up a study scheme for her. This scheme, entitled *De Ratione Studii Puerilis,* "a scheme of juvenile reading," banned all amusing romances and fairy tales as harmful (*"libri pestiferi"*). Instead, Mary was to work through a list which, apart from a good deal of the Bible, included the following:

Plato,
Cicero,
Seneca (*The Maxims*),
Plutarch,
Erasmus (*The Paraphrases*),
Horace (selected poems),
St. Augustine,
St. Jerome,

and a number of other writers, admirable enough, but on the heavy side for a seven-year-old. Vives was possibly reckoning that Mary would be eight, or even nine, before she got through them all.

It would be a mistake to think that her childhood was one long miserable poring over her studies. She loved music and dancing, and there was plenty of both in every Tudor household. She took part in the plays and masques. We hear of one masque, given in the Queen's apartments, when the curtains parted to reveal Mary, with other ladies of the court, in a shining cavern made of cloth of gold, guarded by plumed gentlemen with upraised torches. Mary wore her red hair in a golden net, surmounted by a velvet cap and a garland of jewels. She stayed up dancing with the others until the sun rose—it was May, after all, and she was by then eleven, though the Vicomte de Turenne noted that she was "so thin, spare, and small, as to make it impossible to be married for the next three years."

She had already been more than once betrothed to foreign royalties with whom her father wished to bargain, but none of these engagements had come to anything.

This was a happy time in Mary's life. She had been made Princess of Wales when she was only six, an unusual honor for a girl—the title "Prince of Wales" is often not given to a king's eldest son until he is well in his teens, and that of "Princess" is kept for his wife when he marries.* She, however, was given not only the title, but a great household of three hundred people, under her own chamberlain, with a bishop as the president of her Council, a chancellor, a treasurer, and a long list of other high-sounding officers. With all these fine gentle-

* Thus, the present Queen of England was never Princess of Wales, and her son, Prince Charles, did not automatically become Prince of Wales on his mother's accession. It rests entirely with the sovereign when this title is given.

men and their ladies, she held court in the magnificent castle of Ludlow, where, a century later, Milton was to produce his masque, *Comus.*

It was a beautiful country, with the rolling woods and hills of Shropshire all round, and the long purple band of the Welsh mountains hemming the western sky. From here the little Princess must ride north and south along the Marches, or boundaries, of her principality—north to Chester, where the fat, silver salmon leaped and flashed from the Dee, below the city walls, and south through the orchard lands of Herefordshire and the Forest of Dean to Tewkesbury at the meeting place of Severn and Avon, or Gloucester where, at high tide, one could catch the salty tang of the open sea.

This is still one of the finest countrysides in England, famed for its castles and abbeys and the half-timbered "black-and-white" houses which are specially plentiful in the West Midlands and the Marches. It must have been lovely indeed when Mary rode through it in the fifteen-twenties, when those houses were being built, when the forests were uncut and the castles not yet ruins, and abbeys such as Tintern rang with music and song, where now is only the twitter of birds nesting among cracked masonry.

This sunny opening chapter in Mary's life was over all too soon. She was never to be so carefree again.

The one fact everyone knows about her father is that he had six wives. Many people remember that, and no more, bringing down the tragedy of the Tudors to the level of a rather cheap and obvious joke. Henry is thought of as a character, at once comical and cruel, who outdid the Hollywood film stars in the number of his marriages. But, in actual fact, the motives driving him on were much more complicated than those of Hollywood.

Henry—and his people—passionately wanted a prince to succeed him. Henry's father, Henry VII, had (to be truthful) usurped the throne after the War of the Roses, the bloodiest civil war in English history. Nobody wanted that again. There must be a man to govern England firmly at home—and a man, too, who could stand up to kings and emperors and popes abroad.

Mary had been a disappointment, yet she had been sincerely welcomed, for she was the first of five babies to survive. Next time, every one felt sure, it would be a boy. But the years went by, and there was no next time. It became obvious that Henry and Catherine would never have another child.

By the time Mary was ten, her father was beginning to wonder whether his marriage to Catherine could not somehow be ended, leaving him free to marry again and so perhaps have the son he needed. Put like that, it sounds a cold-blooded suggestion, but it is only fair to study it from all points of view.

Some people see Henry as an entirely selfish brute of a man, sweeping everything and everybody aside to achieve his own desires. Others see him as a conscientious, patriotic ruler, dutifully working his way through a series of marriages in an attempt to provide England with her next king.

The truth, as usual, is probably between the two.

Certainly, Henry's behavior to both Catherine and Mary, from this date onward, seems almost unbelievably brutal. Modern doctors, after studying all that is known about his health, think that a definite change came over his character about 1527, partly as the result of a serious injury to his head a year or two before, when jousting with the Duke of Suffolk, and partly owing to the painful ulcers which afflicted his legs from then until the end of his life. His grim moods and violent rages may be explained, and perhaps excused, in this way.

It must be remembered, too, that divorce, as we understand it today, was unknown in the sixteenth century. The Church was still all-powerful in such matters. In theory, only death could end a marriage. In practice, there was one other way out—for the Church to decide that the marriage *was* no marriage, because it should never have taken place. This way out was open if it was discovered afterward that the man and woman were distantly related, within the "prohibited degrees." Strictly speaking, even the remotest cousins could be disqualified on these grounds, and if the rule had been applied, marriage would have become almost impossible between the royal families of Europe. So usually the rule was ignored, but it remained in the background and was occasionally appealed to when a noble marriage turned out badly.

Now, after many years, the King began to feel

stings of conscience. Queen Catherine had, long ago, been married to his elder brother, Arthur—though only in name, for Arthur had died in boyhood and no one at the time had regarded the "marriage" as completed, least of all young Henry when, in due course, he inherited not only the crown but the wife originally intended for Arthur. About 1526, somewhat late in the day, he began to wonder if, after all, Catherine should not have been counted as Arthur's "widow"—in which case he himself had broken the rules of the Church by attempting to marry his sister-in-law.

There was gossip among the courtiers long before any public announcement. Mary must have heard some of it. She was probably puzzled at first by the whispers concerning her father's new love affair with Anne Boleyn. All her life, Mary remained a very innocent-minded person. Once, even when she was Queen, she horrified her ladies by using a coarse word she had picked up without the least knowledge of its real meaning.

But the most innocent young girl could not be blind to what followed, and soon enough she was forced to feel as well as to see.

Her father's attitude to her, as well as to her mother, completely changed. She was scarcely allowed to come near him, and she was not even given the consolation of living with the Queen.

The Pope refused to dissolve the marriage. Henry did what no English king had ever succeeded in doing before: he defied the Pope. Driven on by his three demons—passion for Anne Boleyn, desire for a son, and the nagging pains of his injury and ill-health—he trampled down all opposition. An English court gave him the divorce which Rome denied him. He married Anne and proclaimed her Queen of England.

So, at sixteen, Mary found that the mother she adored was cast off and disgraced by the father she had always revered. Since it was declared that they had never been legally married, she herself could no longer be regarded as their lawful child. Then came messengers to tell her that she was no longer Princess of Wales. That title now belonged to the baby girl just born to Anne Boleyn and christened Elizabeth.

Catherine faced the new situation with a dignity worthy of her Spanish blood—and, though separated from Mary and forced even to write secret letters to her, she helped her daughter to do the same.

"Daughter," she wrote, "I heard such tidings today that I do perceive, if it be true, the time is come that Almighty God will prove you, and I am very glad of it, for I trust He doth handle you with a good love. I beseech you agree to his pleasure with a merry heart, and be sure that, without fail, he will not suffer you to perish if you beware to offend him. . . . We never come to the Kingdom of Heaven but by troubles. . . . Your loving mother, Catherine the Queen."

Catherine the Queen. . . . Never, throughout her life, would she renounce that title. Mary, inspired by her, clung obstinately to her own title, Princess of Wales, even when for a time she was forced to go and serve as maid of honor to the baby who had taken her place. That was just one of the King's acts of petty bullying. He could not break Catherine's will and make her acknowledge that the marriage between them had never existed. He hoped to be more successful with Mary, but he was disappointed. For Mary, like her mother, offered him all love, respect, and obedience, except in the one vital matter of her conscience.

Both Catherine and Mary went in fear of being poisoned. There is little doubt that, if Henry had been a completely inhuman monster, he could have arranged the removal of either or both. He did not do so. But neither could be sure, at the time, that he would not. The fear hung over them, and it was not lightened for Mary when her own two trusted maids were dismissed and replaced by a single servant girl, a stranger who had no instructions to taste her young mistress's food (as was the custom) before offering it to her. When her mother died, a year or two later, many people firmly believed that she had been poisoned.

Why did Mary make no attempt to escape?

The answer is that she did. She had a powerful friend abroad in Emperor Charles V and was in constant, secret, and dangerous communication with Chapuys, his ambassador in England. A plan was made. The Emperor would send some of his galleons to lie off the mouth of the Thames. Mary, then at Greenwich Palace, would be taken down to the river and put into a boat. It must be a rowing boat, to be independent of wind and tide, but it must carry enough armed men to fight its way through to the open sea.

Before the plan could be carried out, Mary got orders to move to another house, twelve miles from the river. She suggested going there on horseback, perhaps with some desperate idea of breaking away from her escort, but she was made to travel in a litter.

On arrival at the other house, she considered the possibilities of breaking out during the night, but she was too carefully guarded. Her next idea was that, as soon as the weather improved, she should take a country walk in daylight, and that horsemen should appear, pretend to kidnap her against her will, set her on a spare horse, and ride with her to a boat waiting in the river mouth. Before this could be attempted, Mary fell ill and nearly died. When she recovered, the plan was not revived. One difficulty was that Charles, with all the other worries of the Holy Roman Empire on his shoulders, was not so anxious for Mary to leave England as she was herself. He wished her well, but, as a penniless exile in Europe, she would have been just another responsibility. He preferred her to stay where she was, if possible.

Catherine died in 1536. Five months later Anne Boleyn followed her, by way of the scaffold, Henry's desperate method of ridding himself of her. It was now the turn of little Elizabeth to be declared illegitimate and to lose the Welsh title she scarcely understood. Mary and her half sister became companions in misfortune, though Elizabeth had one advantage: being only three years old, she could have little notion of what was happening. Their father married Jane Seymour, who was kind to them and might have proved a sympathetic stepmother. But within the year Jane Seymour died, twelve days after the birth of Edward, the prince so long desired.

Mary was always fond of children. She was fond even of Elizabeth, though she knew no words black enough for her mother, Anne Boleyn. We read of the presents she gave her young sister—twenty shillings in money and, one Christmas, five yards of yellow satin—and how, in the days of Elizabeth's disgrace, she wrote to their father praising her, as "such a child . . . as I doubt not but your highness shall have cause to rejoice of in time coming, as knoweth Almighty God." It must have been easier to love her new brother, for Jane Seymour's marriage had followed her own mother's death, and even Mary could accept it as lawful.

Meanwhile, other things had been happening in England besides royal births, marriages, and deaths.

Henry's defiance of the Pope had exploded all the gathering Protestant feeling in the country. Other nations in Northern Europe were, of course, going Protestant about the same time—it was not simply Henry's divorce which brought the Reformation to England, but it was the match which sent up the powder barrel.

Mary, devout Catholic that she was, all her life,

was now horrified to see her father setting himself up as "Head of the Church" in defiance of Rome. Soon she saw the monasteries dissolved—monks and nuns turned out, abbots bullied or bought into submission (or martyred when they held out), and the King's friends scrambling greedily for the Church lands. New, upstart families set themselves up on the plunder, building mansions with the stones and lead roofing stripped from abbeys and priories, and surrounding them with stolen estates. Ordinary people stood aside, not daring to say much openly, but murmuring scornful little rhymes which are still remembered, such as:

"Wyndham, Popham, Horner, Thynne,
When the monks went out, they went in."

Horner was immortalized in a more familiar rhyme, the hidden meaning of which was clear to all who chuckled over it:

"Little Jack Horner sat in a corner,
Eating his Christmas pie.
He put in his thumb, and pulled out a plum,
And said, 'What a good boy am I!' "

Mary, now a rather sad, serious young woman of twenty, was not one to get much comfort from bitter little retorts such as these. She was too conscious of the empty cloisters and the poor people turned away hungry from the abbey gates where once they had been given charity; of the once lovely churches and chapels, stripped and roofless; and of the crude insults which (to her way of thinking) were everywhere being offered to Christ and His Mother.

She never tried to understand the Reformation. She never had read any of the books and pamphlets which sincere and learned men had written in criticism of the Church. She closed her mind to all such ideas, and thought it was her duty to do so. All she knew was that the English had gone mad and were destroying everything that was best and most holy in life. Someday, God willing, they must be led back to sanity and the true Faith. But who was to do it?

It did not seem likely that it could ever be she.

True, though her father had three more wives, he had no more children, and, as Edward was a delicate little boy, the King was forced to bring Mary back into favor a little. If anything happened to Edward, she was next in line of succession. Whatever the legal rights and wrongs of his first two marriages, Henry had to make the best of things. Edward, Mary, Elizabeth . . . they were all his children, after all. Better one of them than anyone else. So, during the last years of his life, he treated Mary more kindly, and she led a bearable life, sometimes appearing at court but more often living quietly on one of her own manors in the eastern counties. She had pleasure from her music, her reading, her needlework, and her various pets, which included a spaniel, two hounds, and some cage birds. When, on a January day in 1547, Henry lay dying in Whitehall Palace, he sent for her. She knelt beside his bed, and he said, with tears: "Daughter, fortune has been hard against thee, and I grieve I did not have thee married as I wished. . . . I pray thee, try to be a mother to thy brother, for look, he is very little yet."

Mary was not given much chance, however, to look after Edward. The nine-year-old King was in the hands of a Council of Regency, consisting of his uncle, Edward Seymour, and fifteen other members of the new ruling class, not one of whom held a title dating back before the Tudors. Nearly all were ardent reformers. They were determined that the boy should be brought up a Protestant and that the Reformation should be pushed forward in England even more violently than it had been in the old King's time.

The result was a conflict as bitter as that which racks our own century over the question of Communism. Many of our own evils today—censorship and dictatorship, armed risings and brutal reprisals—can be matched, on a smaller scale, in Tudor England. It was no longer just a case of pulling down the crucifix and setting up the Royal Arms in the church, of putting English in the place of Latin, and of splashing whitewash over religious wall paintings. Blood flowed. Priests were hanged from their own church steeples. On both sides, good men did atrocious things in the heat of their passion. America has been fortunate indeed to escape bloodshed over differences in religion, especially since such differences do exist and have played their part in her history—notably in the Puritan settlement of

New England, the Roman Catholic foundation of Maryland, and the various immigrations of French Huguenots, Northern Irish Presbyterians, English Quakers, and other minorities. In America, though, there was space to "live and let live," and these factors operated happily, helping to create a richer and greater nation. In looking back upon the bitterer, more tragic solutions worked out in the cramped area of England, we should try to understand the rival viewpoints of men who honestly could not, by their own lights, see any other way.

Mary, living quietly in one of her country houses, could not entirely keep out of the struggle.

While bowing to her father's orders, she had never forsaken her Catholic faith, and he had never pressed her too far. Now it was forbidden to celebrate the Mass anywhere in the kingdom. Even the King's sister must not let her chaplain conduct the service behind closed doors in the privacy of her own chapel.

Mary ignored the ban. She was a deeply religious woman. To deprive her of the Mass was almost to deprive her of life itself. Her chaplain continued to celebrate Mass accordingly, and—as though by coincidence—her visitors were always most numerous at the appointed times. Gentlemen and humbler folk traveled miles to attend a service which was banned in their own parish churches.

At first she was not seriously interfered with. But there were fanatics in the Council who could not be happy so long as a single person in the country was left to worship God, undisturbed, in her own way. Letters were sent, commissioners descended upon the household. . . . Mary stood up to them. Mass continued to be said in her private chapel, but the net was slowly tightening.

Again she considered the idea of escaping. Life in England was becoming more and more intolerable. Better, surely, the most poverty-stricken exile in a foreign land where her Church was free?

She moved to another of her manors at Woodham Walter, two miles from Maldon, which stands on the Blackwater, one of those tidal rivers which cut up the muddy coast of Essex into a maze of broad estuaries and winding creeks. At that time this lonely region, though within fifty miles of London, was the haunt of Scottish pirates—a fact which, she decided, might be turned to advantage. What could be more natural than that her friend, the Holy Roman Emperor, who was at war with the Scots, should send a squadron of warships to hunt them on the Essex coast?

A plan was worked out and put into operation. The Emperor's Flemish admiral, Scepperus, hovered offshore with seven vessels, while an eighth sailed to within five miles of Maldon. A rowing boat was sent upriver to the town itself with an elaborate story about a cargo of grain to be sold locally. This was to disarm suspicion. Dubois, who had been secretary to the ambassador, Chapuys, and was now acting as the Emperor's agent in this matter, slipped up to the churchyard overlooking the quay. Here, by arrangement, he met Sir Robert Rochester, comptroller of Mary's household, to discuss how she might be got away.

So far, the story runs like a historical novel. But escapes in real life bristle with extra difficulties ignored by the novelist.

We are apt to think that trade restrictions and government interference are a modern invention. Our newspapers and politicians invite us to look back to "the good old days" when a man could do as he liked with his own. But, when we study social history in detail, we find that the merchants of bygone days suffered from plenty of official regulations too. Dubois' consignment of grain brought so many awkward questions from the Maldon authorities—the customs, the bailiff, and so on—that he must have cursed the day when he thought of the idea.

Precious time was lost over this and other hesitations. Dubois saw how difficult it would be to get Mary down to the boat unobserved. A great deal was at stake. This was not a simple question of rescuing a private person—great political issues were implicit in it. If the rescue succeeded, there would be trouble enough. If it failed, the consequences for Mary might be disastrous.

Dubois suggested they should risk it. Sir Robert Rochester said it was impossible. "They are going to double the watch tonight," he said, "and post men on the church tower—a thing that has never been done before. All we can do is to see to getting *you* out of this."

Mary kept repeating, miserably: "What is to become of me? What is to become of me?" It was one of the moments in her life when her courage deserted her. As Dubois rode away in the darkness she must have felt hopeless indeed.

As things turned out, Dubois passed the watch and reached his boat without any trouble. If Mary had been with him in disguise she would probably have escaped. In which case, she might have lived longer and more happily, but it is unlikely that she would ever have reigned over England.

The attempt was never made, but Mary's enemies in the Council were well aware that it had been planned, and she was made to suffer for it. Edward, prompted by them, asked her if it was true, as it was rumored, that she still regularly heard Mass. Mary burst into tears. The boy, who was softhearted and emotional, and fond of the grown-up sister who had always been kind to him, was so upset that he too shed tears. The awkward moment passed, but the Council were not going to let her escape so lightly. Soon she received a letter from the King. Possibly the boy found it easier to write than to speak to her face. Possibly, too, the Council found it easier to dictate the written word.

"Truly, sister," wrote Edward, "I will not say more or worse things, because my duty would compel me to use harsher and angrier words. But this I will say with certain intention, that I will see my laws strictly obeyed, and those who break them shall be watched and denounced. . . ."

This time Mary did not answer with tears. When

her letters achieved nothing, and more threats were made to her, she rode to London and confronted Edward in the midst of his Council. There, without a single friend to support her, she faced the twenty-five councillors, who bayed at her like a pack of hounds. But all their shouting could not quell her spirit.

The King, she said firmly, was too young yet to decide such deep questions of religion. "He is of great understanding," she admitted, remembering what a studious boy he had always been, "but experience will teach him more yet." It was a true elder sister's remark, more true than tactful, and Edward was stung to retort as any other boy might have done: *"You* may still have something to learn —no one is too old for that!" The argument rolled on, until Mary summed up the simple issue. "There are two things only, soul and body. My soul I offer to God, and my body to Your Majesty's service." That was the unyielding answer she had always given to her father and the only one she could ever give. She added, with deep feeling: "May it please you to take away my life rather than the old religion!"

More than once in the months which followed she repeated her willingness to die for her faith. At last the Council were able to stop the celebration of Mass in her household, but even they could not force her to use the new Protestant Prayer Book. She told the Bishop of London, Ridley, who was later to be burned for his beliefs: "The door of the parish church adjoining shall be open for you if you come; and you may preach if you will; but neither I, nor any of mine, shall hear you." The Council bullied her no further. They had fresh cares on their minds.

In the new year—1553, that was—Edward caught a feverish chill from which he never properly recovered. All through that spring the boy was slowly dying of tuberculosis. The Tudors were prone to that disease, and the sixteen-year-old boy had never grown strong enough to fight it.

The Duke of Northumberland had taken Seymour's place by now and was almost the dictator of England. He saw that the whole basis of his power was rocking. Who would succeed to the throne? By rights, under Henry VIII's will, it should be Mary, who would undo all that the Reformation had accomplished. At all costs, the Duke decided, that must never happen.

Who else, then? By a strange coincidence the next six persons in line for the crown (which had never been left to a female since Maud's day) were all women. There was the nineteen-year-old Elizabeth; Edward's cousin, the Duchess of Suffolk, and her daughter, Lady Jane Grey, now sixteen; and, among others, a second Mary, later famous as the Queen of Scots.

If Mary Tudor was to be set aside at all, the Duke felt he might as well make himself thoroughly safe. He resolved to pass over Elizabeth as well. The two sisters were not sufficiently unfriendly for him to play off one against the other, and Elizabeth was too moderate in her Protestant views. She was too grown-up, besides, and too strong a character. Jane Grey was more manageable.

On Whit Sunday, the Duke's second son, Lord Guilford Dudley, was married to her. On the eleventh of June the dying boy informed the crown lawyers that they were to prepare a will, changing the succession. If his cousin, the Duchess of Suffolk, had a son during his own lifetime, that son was to inherit the throne; otherwise, her daughter Jane. . . .

They had only to look at the boy's flushed face to know what that meant. There was no time for sons. Jane would be Queen within a few weeks or months at most. And, since that Whitsun wedding, her father-in-law would be more truly master of England than ever before.

It was useless—and dangerous—to protest. The will was made. The Duke continued with his plans. Arms were collected. All kinds of pretenses were kept up so that the seriousness of the King's illness should be hidden from the people. Rumors circulated that he was dead. To contradict them, the Duke forced Edward to show himself at the palace windows, though he had to be held up from behind. That was only two days before he died. Even afterward, his death was kept secret for another three days. The Duke needed all the time he could get to put his scheme into operation.

Mary was to be arrested before she could move a finger. She was, just then, at Hunsdon House near Hertford, some way north of London. The house was watched. At the first sign of flight, she could be seized.

However, the Duke evidently thought it would be better if she could be got to walk into the trap of her own accord. As Edward lay dying, word was sent to both Mary and Elizabeth to come to Greenwich and see him. Elizabeth wisely found excuses to delay. Mary set out and rode as far as Hoddesdon. There she was met by an unknown messenger who had ridden posthaste to warn her that her brother was already dead.

Mary had to think quickly. Clearly the Council could not be meaning to proclaim her Queen. If they were, she would have been summoned to the palace long ago, and the seriousness of Edward's illness would not have been hidden from her. Nor would she now be hearing of his death unofficially—there should have been noble messengers kneeling before her, kissing her hand, and saluting her as Queen.

What *was* happening? What was Elizabeth doing? It was impossible to be sure of anything. She must, somehow, play for time. And, whatever happened, she must avoid arrest.

It was already night. Taking only two of her women and half a dozen of her gentlemen as escort, she turned and rode north along the Newmarket road. The cordon of watchers round Hunsdon House had given up their vigil when they saw her start for London. None saw her turn in her tracks and make for the greater safety of one of her Norfolk manors. The Duke's own cleverness, in trying to lure her to London, had given her the means of escape.

At dawn she paused to rest and hear Mass in the

house of a loyal Catholic supporter. Then, disguised and riding pillion behind one of his servants, she pressed on. Sixty miles of hard riding brought her to Hengrave Hall, exhausted but for the moment safe. A few days later she moved to the greater security of Framlingham Castle in Suffolk.

It seemed, for the moment, that the Duke of Northumberland held all the cards in his hand—except Mary herself.

He had been preparing his stroke for months. He had troops and arms, and a fleet mobilized in the Thames. He dominated the Council, which was assembled in the Tower of London—its members practically his prisoners and unable to oppose him. Mary had no supporters organized and did not know who would help her. She nearly despaired and thought to take ship from Yarmouth, to escape abroad while she could. But she stayed to see the matter out.

The Duke pressed on with his plans. Lady Jane Grey was proclaimed Queen. He wanted to proclaim his son king at the same time, but the girl suddenly showed that she had a will of her own. She would make her husband a duke, but no more.

Then, amazingly, the whole revolution collapsed. It is hard to say quite why, except that, during the long years since Maud and Stephen, the English people had developed a strong sense of law. No longer did they follow their leaders blindly into battle. The people knew that Mary was the rightful Queen. Even the average Protestant felt it was better to have her, Catholic though she was. If kings and queens were to be chosen on their merits, there might be a civil war every time the sovereign died. The crown was something which should pass by law, whatever people thought of its wearer as an individual.

Gentlemen got out their armor, looked to their pistols, and crowded the roads to Mary's headquarters. Having no other general he could trust to deal with them, the Duke himself set out at the head of his troops. But, as he rode, dispatches of disaster overtook him at every milestone. Mary had been proclaimed Queen in the West Country, in Cheshire on the Welsh Marches, and—dangerously near—in Buckinghamshire. The fleet in the Thames had gone over to her side. His fellow councillors, once his back was turned, had come out of the Tower and proclaimed her in London itself. "Queen Jane" was a prisoner.

By the time Northumberland reached Cambridge, he knew the game was up. Beneath his domineering exterior, the dictator was a miserable coward at heart. At Cambridge, in a despairing effort to cover up the treason of the past months, he himself proclaimed Mary Queen. It did not save him. He was at once arrested, and in due course, though he groveled for mercy and experienced a sudden and convenient conversion to the old religion, he was beheaded on Tower Hill.

Only two others, ringleaders with him, were put to death. Though Mary has gone down in legend as "Bloody Mary" she was actually of a merciful disposition—far more so than her supporters thought safe and desirable. Certainly she had no intention, at this time, of putting Jane Grey, or even her husband, to death.

Meanwhile, amid noisy rejoicings, she rode triumphantly into London. Elizabeth met her outside the city. They kissed and rode forward side by side.

The younger sister had wisely kept clear of all that had been happening in recent days. Ever since she could remember, Elizabeth had lived in a world of danger and uncertainty. She had the wisdom of the tree which bends to the wind. Mary could never bend. Her mind was rigid. A thing was either right or wrong: if it was wrong, why not say so? She was no good at pretenses, and she was impatient of delays. Elizabeth, on the other hand, was excellent at pretenses—she had just been pretending to be ill, to avoid coming to London until the crisis was over, one way or another. And she was, all her life, a mistress of the delaying action.

The contrast between the two sisters was never more obvious than it now became.

Mary's one idea was to restore England to the Roman faith, to undo every act of the Reformation, and to ensure that never again should the country lapse into Protestant heresy.

The Holy Roman Emperor, with his seat in Vienna, begged her to go slowly and tactfully. Let her begin by hearing Mass herself and giving the same liberty to others who wanted it, but let her remember that a great part of her subjects were Protestants and they would not change overnight.

Mary could see no sense in such worldly wisdom. The old faith, she felt, was true, the new one was false and abominable. Her heretic subjects must be rescued from it for their own good. So, in the shortest possible time, the churches must be restored to their old appearance, the monks and nuns and friars must return, everything must be as it was when she was a girl. There was only one thing even Mary dared not attempt: to take back the Church lands from the families which now held them. Her Council and Parliament were ready to accept everything else, but the pockets of the new nobility and middle class (their own pockets, in many cases) must not be touched.

On September 30, Mary was crowned at Westminster, the first woman in history to undergo that ceremony as sovereign. She wore a mantle of crimson velvet, furred with ermine, and a long gown of white taffeta underneath. She was belted with a sword, and spurs were even fitted on her feet, for the procedure as closely as possible followed the coronation of a king. As Cranmer, the Archbishop of Canterbury, was a stanch Protestant, the crown was put on her head by the Bishop of Winchester.

As the procession moved out at the end of the long, exhausting ceremony, Elizabeth was heard to whisper to the French ambassador that she had found her own coronet uncomfortable. "Have patience," hissed the Frenchman, "it is only preparation for one that will rest more easily!"

That was the prospect which haunted Mary. She was now thirty-seven and by no means healthy. If anything happened to her, Elizabeth would succeed —and all the work she had done to restore the old religion might be undone once more. Elizabeth had been brought up a Protestant. Now she was attending Mass and offering to study Catholic books with an open mind, to see if she could accept their teaching. But how far was she sincere? How far was it another of her famous delaying actions? Even when someone remarked that she had not looked very happy during Mass, Elizabeth had unblushingly brought out the schoolgirl excuse that she had been suffering from stomach-ache at the time! Though not worldly-wise, Mary was, after all, her sister; and she was beginning to suspect these convenient little illnesses which came upon Elizabeth at critical moments.

Elizabeth was dangerous. As Renard said—he was now the Emperor's ambassador and Mary's close adviser—Elizabeth had "a power of enchantment." How many of her subjects were to know it in the next half century!

There was only one way to checkmate Elizabeth and keep England safe for the old religion. Mary must marry and have an heir. Once she had come to this conclusion, she pushed the scheme forward with furious determination, in spite of all warnings. She would marry the Emperor's son, Philip of Spain —that same Philip who, thirty-five years later, was to hurl the Armada against Elizabeth.

The whole idea of a Spanish marriage was most

unpopular with her people. Though Drake at this moment was only a little boy, and Raleigh scarcely out of his cradle, there was already plenty of ill-feeling between the two countries. The result was a conspiracy, with links in many parts of England, though only in Kent did it flare up into mass rebellion. Here Sir Thomas Wyatt mustered a large force and marched to London Bridge, which was closed against him. London was in an uproar. Mary rode down to the Guildhall to meet the Lord Mayor and make an appeal for loyalty.

Normally she had none of that "power of enchantment" already noted in Elizabeth. But that afternoon she rose to the occasion, just as Elizabeth did long afterward when she reviewed her troops at Tilbury, in the shadow of the Armada. If the two speeches are compared, a rather similar ring may be noticed in the phrasing.

"I am come unto you in mine own person," said Mary, "to tell you that which already you see and know; that is, how traitorously and rebelliously a number of Kentishmen have assembled themselves against us and you. . . . And I say to you on the word of a prince, I cannot tell how naturally the mother loveth the child, for I was never the mother of any; but certainly, if a prince and governor may as naturally and earnestly love her subjects as the mother doth love the child, then assure yourselves that I, being your lady and mistress, do as earnestly and tenderly love and favor you. And I, thus loving you, cannot but think that ye as heartily and faithfully love me. And then I doubt not but that we shall give these rebels a short and speedy overthrow."

Twenty thousand enrolled under her banner after this appeal. Wyatt, unable to force London Bridge, crossed the Thames higher up and burst into the city. For some hours there was panic, with skirmishing all over what is now the West End of London, and arrows flying at Charing Cross within range of Whitehall Palace, where Mary (by someone's mismanagement or treachery) had only a few gentlemen-pensioners to guard her. But the rebels were not sufficiently determined. Many of them melted away in the confusion, and by the end of the day Wyatt was a prisoner in the Tower.

The whole business had given Mary and her supporters a fright. Not only was Wyatt put to death but so were Lady Jane Grey and her husband. They had been in prison all this time, formally under sentence of death for their treason but actually (had it not been for Wyatt's revolt) in no great danger of execution. Now Mary hardened her heart.

Even Elizabeth was in greater danger than ever. If Wyatt had succeeded, he would have put her on the throne. How far, Mary wondered, had her sister been in the plot herself? Needless to say, Elizabeth had created a strong alibi. She had been staying quietly at Ashridge all the time—and not feeling in the best of health. Mary had her doubts about that. She summoned her to court, thoughtfully sending her own litter and two doctors, so that Elizabeth might have the closest medical supervision. Even so, the resourceful Princess managed to take five days over the short journey and to make a dramatic appearance in the London streets, dressed entirely in white and winning a most sympathetic welcome from the crowd. Before long she was under arrest and in the Tower. The old friendship between the half sisters was dead.

Mary went ahead with her plans to marry Philip. She had begun in a cold spirit of duty, but soon she began to have warmer feelings. There had been so little affection in her sad life. Always, she had been lonely and afraid. Now at last she was to have the companionship of a husband and perhaps children of her own.

Philip sailed from Corunna with a fleet of a hundred and fifty ships and landed at Southampton in July, where it poured with rain to greet him. It was the welcome which the Spaniards expected. They were well aware that England did not want them. "Know ye," Philip warned his staff, "I am going not to a marriage feast but to a fight!" He was not looking forward to the future, as Mary was. He was ten years younger than she. She was nearing forty and sorrow had made her look older. She was thin and frail now, so shortsighted that she had to lift books and papers to within a few inches of her nose, and she kept her lips tightly pursed. To a modern eye she would have seemed almost elderly.

Bride and groom met for the first time at the Bishop's Palace in Winchester. Mary wore cloth of silver, with a close-fitting cap of black and gold, and a good deal of jewelry, of which she was always very fond. Philip was in white, with magnificent trimmings of gold and silver. Mary took his hand, Philip kissed her on the mouth—he knew it was the English custom, often remarked upon by foreign visitors, to be very free with kisses in public—and he tactfully paid the same compliment to all her ladies as they were introduced. Philip spoke in Spanish. Mary understood him, but could not answer fluently in that language, so she talked French. The first meeting went off very well.

Two days later they were married in Winchester Cathedral. Mary's wedding dress was of white satin, heavy with jewels. A mantle of gold hung from her shoulders. Scarlet shoes peeped from below her skirt as she rustled down the aisle to where Philip, equally glorious in white satin and cloth of gold, awaited her on a high platform built in the middle of the church.

So that Philip should not be inferior in rank to his bride, his father the Emperor that day created him King of Naples. So, when the trumpets pealed at the end of the marriage service, Mary heard herself and her husband proclaimed with a string of titles perhaps longer than any ever shared by an English queen before or since: "Philip and Mary, by the grace of God King and Queen of England, France, Naples, Jerusalem and Ireland, Defenders of the Faith, Princes of Spain and Sicily, Archdukes of Austria, Dukes of Milan, Burgundy and Brabant, Counts of Habsburg, Flanders and Tyrol. . . ."

How vain was all that glory Mary had just time to learn in the few years of life which were left to her.

Little more than four remained. Her whole reign lasted only five and a half years, and there was nothing much in it of importance to us today. What *is* generally remembered now? That she won the nickname "Bloody Mary" for persecuting the Protestants . . . and that she said, when she was dying, that the word "Calais" would be found written on her heart.

Apart from those who died on the scaffold as rebels, there were about three hundred persons burned at the stake as heretics when the restored Church brought the Inquisition into England. Of these, a few—Cranmer, Latimer, Ridley—were bishops, but none of the others was well known. They were humble working people mainly, from London and the southeastern counties. Smithfield, outside the walls of the capital, was the favorite scene for the burnings, though the martyrdom of the bishops took place at Oxford. Of all the upper class who had so willingly enriched themselves with monastery lands, not one went to the stake for refusing to turn Catholic again. Mary, when weak herself, had begged for freedom to worship God in her own way, and as Queen she refused that freedom to others. But it is only fair to her memory to say that, if Protestants were persecuted by her, Catholics suffered just as harshly under the other Tudors. In that century neither side believed in liberty for its enemies.

The loss of Calais seemed, at the time, more serious than it really was.

For two hundred years, since the victories of the

great Edward III, England had held a bridgehead on the French coast—Calais and the country round about. Mary's marriage to Philip brought war with France, Spain's enemy. All through this period France favored Elizabeth, as the French ambassador revealed by his remark to her at Mary's coronation. Now, in 1558, the French attacked Calais, and, to the amazement and consternation of everyone in England, the neglected, ill-garrisoned town was taken. The place was not nearly as valuable to England as people imagined, but the shock to the public was tremendous. Mary's popularity sank even lower. It was no wonder that the dying, disappointed woman cried that "Calais" would be written on her heart.

Her great disappointment in those last years was that no children were born to her. She had to face the truth at last: she would have no heir of her own, and the crown must pass to Elizabeth.

To this grief was added another. She had fallen in love with Philip, the husband she had married for reasons of state. But Philip had never been in love with her. And he knew that, though his likeness faced hers on the coins of England, his position in the country would vanish when she died. If she had had a child, he would have kept a good deal of influence. But when no child was born, Philip lost interest in England and Mary alike. He went abroad to see to his continental possessions, and, though Mary was continually bombarding him with letters and appeals, it was a long time before he recrossed the sea to visit her.

On November 17, 1558, she died after a long illness. She had been a good woman but a bad queen. The very strength and sincerity of her religious views, so worthy in a private person, made her unsuitable to govern a population which largely disagreed with them. Despite all the cruelties done in her name, it is impossible not to pity her. As we look back down the centuries, it would be fairer to remember her not wreathed round with the smoke of the heretic fires at Smithfield and Oxford, but sitting in some farmhouse parlor, as she loved to do, chatting with some of the local people who did not even know that she was the Queen, but mistook her for one of her own ladies.

"Mary, Mary, quite contrary,
How does your garden grow?
Silver bells, and cockleshells,
And little maids all in a row?"

A cockleshell was the badge of a pilgrim who had been to Compostella in Spain. The little maids were the nuns whom Mary had brought back into England. They were soon to be uprooted again, for now the garden was Elizabeth's.

ŏŏŏ

THE FIRST ELIZABETH

There are always people to cheer a new monarch, to blow trumpets, pull bell ropes, and touch off cannon, but the frenzy of joy which greeted Elizabeth was genuine indeed. As the Spanish Count de Feria regretfully informed Philip, "She is greatly attached to the people, and quite confident that they are all on her side, which is perfectly true."

Nowhere was she more loved than in London, a city strong in Protestant feeling. Her coronation, fixed for January 15, 1559, was used as a great opportunity of displaying her to the city. First, a few days beforehand, she moved from Whitehall Palace to the Tower, going by water with a pomp and ceremony which (an Italian visitor admitted) rivaled the greatest of state occasions at Venice itself. Then, on the eve of the coronation, she returned to Whitehall in an open litter born by mules, slowly threading the narrow streets and pausing frequently to accept a bouquet or a sprig of rosemary, to smile at the Latin compliments showered on her by some schoolboy orator, and to glance at the "pageants" or living tableaux set up on stages at intervals along the route.

One of these had Father Time as its central figure.

"Time!" she was heard to comment. "And Time hath brought me hither!"

A strange remark from a young woman of twenty-five, who might easily have had to wait another twenty years or more before coming to the throne. . . .

Yet there was a wealth of meaning in it. Time had always been her friend and ally. When in danger, she had always played for time—and always would. And now Time had brought her to the crown of England, though often she had seemed more likely to end upon the block.

Her early life had been similar to Mary's in many ways, different in others.

Like Mary, she was born at Greenwich Palace, on September 7, 1533. But Mary's godfather Wolsey had meantime fallen from favor, and Elizabeth was sponsored by Archbishop Cranmer, leader in the English Reformation.

She could have no real memory of her mother, the dark-eyed, gay, yet calculating Anne Boleyn, for she lost her before she was three years old. So there was none of that powerful influence which Catherine of Aragon had wielded over Mary until she was in her teens. What Elizabeth got from Anne could not have been much more than certain inherited qualities—some of her vivacity, perhaps, and love of pleasure, and a flirtatiousness together with the ability to control her emotions and see clearly ahead.

It is always unwise, however, to be too certain about tracing "inherited qualities." All of these—except the last—were conspicuous in her father also, and could just as well have come from him. And certainly it was her father she always admired and imitated. Elizabeth was far more a Tudor than a Boleyn, but her mother left her one asset there was no denying—English blood. Whereas Mary was half Spanish, Elizabeth could boast that she was "mere English," and won much of her popularity thereby.

Like Mary, she was brought up in country houses away from the court, and had the same Lady Bryan in charge of her early upbringing. But whereas Mary's first years were years of sunshine and glory, with humiliation to follow, Elizabeth lost her high place, with her mother, before she was old enough to realize it. She was only four when she was taken to church and made to hold up the christening robe of the baby brother who had come to displace her. So, at the age when Mary had been holding court at Ludlow Castle, Elizabeth was nobody in particular. Even Lady Bryan did not know (she complained in a letter) what Elizabeth's new position was supposed to be. What was certain was that the girl must have some more clothes—she had practically nothing to wear.

But this phase of neglect did not last long. Soon

(as we have seen in Mary's case) she was largely restored to favor and was given her due place of honor, next after her brother and elder sister. She was thirteen and a half when her father, Henry VIII, died. She had been brought up as a Protestant, so she had none of the bullying which Mary suffered from Edward's Council. For a short time she lived with her stepmother, Catherine Parr, her father's last wife, who had quickly remarried. Her husband was the Lord High Admiral, Thomas Seymour, younger brother of Edward Seymour who, as Lord Protector, dominated the first years of the boy-King's reign.

We know a good deal about this period of Elizabeth's girlhood. We know that she was high-spirited and attractive, with her striking blue eyes, red-gold hair, and clear olive skin. Catherine and Thomas used to burst into her room, fling aside the bed curtains, and tickle her till she rolled and squealed across the bed. On one occasion, in the garden of their riverside house at Chelsea, Catherine held her prisoner while Thomas slashed her dress to shreds. Presumably the joke was taken in good part. Elizabeth's wardrobe was no longer as limited as it had been a few years before.

Fun and games of this type, so different from anything the sober Mary knew, may have been quite innocent, but they caused a great deal of gossip. Thomas Seymour was an ambitious and passionate man. It was known that he would have much preferred to marry a youthful princess (quite possibly a future queen) than a king's widow whose influence must be going down rather than up. It was noticed, too, that the hearty Admiral was quite willing to keep the fun going even when Catherine was not present to take part, and that Elizabeth was apt to go pink when his name was mentioned. The end of it was that at Whitsuntide in the following year it was arranged for the Princess to set up her own household at Cheshunt, in Hertfordshire.

Catherine and she remained good friends, however, and wrote to each other until the end of the summer, when Catherine died in giving birth to a baby. Thomas Seymour, now free again, caused Elizabeth a good deal of embarrassment during the next few months. It was not just that he was anxious to marry her, but he tried to involve her in treasonable plots against the government. Elizabeth, however, had sense beyond her years. She was attracted to this man and flattered by his attentions, but, even at fifteen, she was developing a kind of controlling caution. Her own mother had died on the scaffold for alleged treason—and it was to the scaffold that Thomas was sent by his own brother, the following March, on the same charge. There was suspicion against Elizabeth, but no proof. She breathed again and thanked Heaven she had not been led into any of his wildcat schemes.

It had been a narrow escape, but also a valuable lesson. She was to remember it later, in Mary's reign, especially during the Wyatt affair.

We should have quite a false picture of Elizabeth's girlhood if we merely imagined her romping and laughing with Thomas Seymour and her stepmother. All through that time she was studying hard. She had a better brain than Mary and was a finer scholar.

She was learning French, Italian, and Latin before she was ten. Then she started Greek, which was becoming fashionable now, as the full force of the Renaissance reached England. Cambridge was the headquarters of the "humanists," as the Greek enthusiasts were called. From this group were to come many of the outstanding figures of Elizabethan England—statesmen such as William Cecil, her principal secretary, and churchmen such as Mathew Parker, the archbishop. Their ideas, inspired by the history and philosophy, the poems and plays of the ancients, were to revolutionize English life in many fields; and in none more than literature and education.

At that moment in time, as the reddish head of Elizabeth bowed over the strange but beautiful Greek characters, English literature as we know it today hardly existed, except for Chaucer. Yet, before she died, she was to see *Hamlet,* and her name was to be associated forever afterward with those of Shakespeare and Spenser, Marlowe and Jonson, Donne and Drayton, and a host of others. As for translations . . . if the schoolgirl Elizabeth had been lazy and sought an easy way through her work, she would have found very few published English versions of the Greek and Latin authors she was studying; but, by the end of her reign, most of the ancient classics were to be available in printed translations for all to read, so that the less scholarly poets like Shakespeare, with his "little Latin and less Greek," should nonetheless be deeply influenced by the new movement.

Elizabeth did not just happen to live during this springtime of English literature; she was part of it. She was inspired by Roger Ascham, the great pioneer of Tudor education, corresponding with him in Latin and even securing him as her tutor for a short time. In a letter to a fellow scholar in Germany, Ascham gives us a glimpse of her at sixteen:

"Her mind has no womanly weakness, her perseverance is equal to that of a man, and her memory long keeps what it quickly picks up. She talks French and Italian as well as she does English, and has often talked to me readily and well in Latin, moderately in Greek. When she writes Greek and Latin, nothing is more beautiful than her handwriting. . . ."

When she was nearly thirty and had been several years a queen, with all the weight of public business to carry, she still made time to read Greek and Latin with him almost every day. In the meantime she had learned Spanish, and we even hear of her discussing fashions in bad German. She was proud of her skill in foreign languages, and with good reason. Not only could she hold her own in the most cultured and scholarly company but she was able to talk directly with foreign ambassadors, none of whom, in those days, thought it necessary to study English. In this way she was able to keep her own finger on affairs of state which otherwise her councilors might have managed to keep in their own hands. That priceless gift of languages enabled her to rule, not merely reign.

Along with all this and other schoolwork, such as mathematics and what passed then as "science," she loved sport. Henry had been a great hunter. So was she. We read of a typical day's sport in the last year of Mary's reign. The Princess was then living at Hatfield, and she rode out in the morning to Enfield Chase, a slender figure, moderately tall, attended by twelve ladies in white satin and twenty yeomen in green—white and green being the Tudor colors. Elizabeth had silver-tipped arrows winged with peacock feathers—but they were not solely for ornament. The elegant huntress rode hard, shot straight, and finished off the wounded buck with her own knife.

She hunted until she was nearly seventy. Every day she rode and walked. She was a keen dancer. In 1589, more than thirty years after she came to the throne, she was accustomed to dance six or seven galliards* as morning exercise. She loved music and singing, as most people did, for hers was the golden age of the madrigal and of such composers as Byrd and Tallis, when England was perhaps the most musical nation in Europe.

This, then, was the kind of girl she was—a student, a sportswoman, warm-blooded in flirtatious romps with Thomas Seymour, coolheaded in political crises which might have stampeded people twice her age.

* A lively new dance, introduced about the year before.

During the five and a half years of her sister's reign she developed into a full-grown woman . . . and a full-grown statesman. Perils surrounded her. She had to play for time, she had to pretend. It is easy for us, remembering her tricks and excuses, remembering above all how she made a show of changing her religion to satisfy Mary, to declare bluntly that she was nothing but a young liar and hypocrite. She was both at times. But she was never "nothing but." Elizabeth was so very much more. It was perhaps better for England that she should lie and live, than perish as a martyr to plain speaking.

We, judging her, know the glory that was round the corner. From her eyes it was hidden. Never, at any moment, could she know for certain that she would live to be Queen. One mistake, one piece of ill-luck, and she would be no more in the chronicles of her country than Lady Jane Grey or the Princes in the Tower. Any one of those royal messengers calling her to London might have been the last. When, with suspicion heaviest upon her, Mary sent her to the Tower, there was at least an even chance that she would never come out alive.

We know now that she did. Mary sent her to live, virtually a prisoner, at Woodstock in Oxfordshire. Captive though she was, she was received all along the route with royal honors. The London merchants saluted her barge with unofficial gunfire. Villagers rang their bells, though they were put in prison for it. When she continued the journey by land, the countrywomen pressed cakes and delicacies upon her until she had to wave them away with a smile. We know now that Elizabeth was already so dearly loved by the people that Mary dared not touch her. Elizabeth could not know that; she could only hope and trust.

The marvel is, not that she showed caution sometimes, but that she was as bold—impudent, almost—as she was at other times. She proved a troublesome captive at Woodstock, and in due course Mary realized it was not worth the bother of holding her there. She came back to court, and later moved to Hatfield. By then she was fairly certain that Mary would never have a child to inherit the crown, and she was more than ever determined to fend off any proposals that she should marry some foreign prince and be shipped abroad. No, at all costs she must hang on. The people wanted her—the least vain of women would have been forced to see that, and Elizabeth was by no means the least vain. It was only a question of time.

And a few months later she could cry from the depths of her heart as the coronation procession halted on its way to Westminster: *"Time! And Time hath brought me hither!"*

Cheering and bell ringing were all very well. When the door was closed on the joyful noises outside, she faced a different picture in the quiet of the Council chamber.

The situation of the country was low indeed. It was summed up in a Council memorandum as follows: "The Queen poor; the realm exhausted; the nobility poor and decayed; good captains and soldiers wanting, the people out of order; justice not executed; all things dear; excesses in meat, diet and apparel: division among ourselves; war with France; the French king bestriding the realm, having one foot in Calais and the other in Scotland; steadfast enemies, but no steadfast friends."

The rest of Elizabeth's life story is the tale of her fight to alter that state of affairs.

Her first action was to choose the man who was to be her lifelong partner in the work—no husband, but her principal secretary. For this key post she chose William Cecil, one of that brilliant group of Cambridge humanists. Grandson of an innkeeper, Cecil was an outstanding example of the "new men" whom Elizabeth brought in to freshen up the "poor and decayed" nobility. Cecil became, in time, Lord Burghley, and founded a family which has been prominent in public life right down to the present day.

"This judgment I have of you," Elizabeth told him, "that you will not be corrupted with any manner of gift, and that you will be faithful to the State, and that without respect of my private will you will give me that counsel that you think best." And so, for the next forty years, he did.

Government in those days was a highly personal matter. In some respects the position of this first Elizabeth was more like that of an American president than a modern English queen. Immense power and responsibility were vested in her. She took advice, but she herself had to decide. There was no question of sitting back as a neutral and signing whatever was laid before her. She turned to Parliament only when necessary, on some vital matter—usually concerned with money. She was no enthusiast for democracy and Parliamentary government. She and Cecil, she felt, knew what they were doing much more clearly than these assemblies of noblemen and country squires. In the circumstances of the late sixteenth century she was quite certainly right.

That, then, was how she ruled. The Council gave advice. Foreign ambassadors she interviewed herself. Her finger was in every pie. Even Cecil began with the idea that some matters should be kept from her, as things which a woman could not be expected to understand; he quickly found his mistake. He learned to sum up the pros and cons of each question and lay them fairly before her, adding his own considered opinion if need be. She made the final decision, right or wrong.

Sometimes, when foreign affairs were at some point of crisis, only Elizabeth and Cecil knew what was happening. He himself put the secret dispatches into code and deciphered the answers. It suited the Queen's temperament. She worked best in the dark.

Needless to say, it was not made obvious to people at the time that she and Cecil were running the country. If Cecil had been a vain or showy personality—like the Earl of Essex, who won so much influence toward the end of her reign—it might have been difficult to hide the true position. But Cecil was no lover of the spotlight for himself, and he never abused his position to further his own ends. Officially he was no more than a member of the Council, and she chose the other members of that Council cleverly. It was a mixture of well-known "safe" names to reassure the public and new blood to revitalize the weakened state.

Reassuring the public was very necessary after the unrest of the past few years. Changes must come, she knew; but she knew also that her Englishmen hated change and were always hankering after what they imagined were "the good old days." How then could she do what she *must* do, if England were to recover and grow great again? The answer she found was to make changes as gently and quietly as possible, never drawing attention to them, halting when she ran into too much opposition, quietly going forward again as the indignation died down. People, she knew, had short memories except where their own interests were concerned. They could see the outward form of things, but few were sharp enough to divine the inner meaning.

The first matter on which they had to be reassured was religion.

Mary had asked her to maintain the old faith, without much confidence that she would do so. The Protestants, with the smoke of Smithfield still bitter in their nostrils, wanted revenge and a return to the Reformation. Most ordinary folk just wanted peace and an end to this seesaw movement.

"Division among ourselves. . . ." Elizabeth

wanted to abolish that, so that the people, no longer *"out of order,"* might show a united front to their *"steadfast enemies."* How could she satisfy the Protestant majority without setting the Catholic minority against her and making more enemies among the Catholic governments abroad?

She found the answer in the so-called Elizabethan Settlement, a compromise which has lasted to this day and still governs the Church of England. Instead of bringing back the outright Protestant Prayer Book of Edward VI, which Mary had abolished, she instituted the one now used. In this, the all-important Communion service was so blended with the phrasing of the Roman Mass that, to quote one modern historian, "the worshiper may find whichever doctrine he wishes to find."

One thorny question had to be dealt with long before new prayer books could be thought of. Edward, like her father, had included in his royal titles "Supreme Head of the Church." Mary, with her allegiance to the Pope, had dropped the phrase. Everyone waited to see if Elizabeth would put it back. If she did, it would please Protestants—but they were happy enough already—whereas Catholics, both at home and abroad, would receive it as a slap in the face.

Elizabeth found a neat answer, which must have made her chuckle inwardly. In the first public documents she issued, her titles stopped short with an *"etcetera."* People could make what they liked of that. She was not showing her whole hand until she had to.

"War with France; the French king bestriding the realm, having one foot in Calais and the other in Scotland . . ."

We are so used to reading about the Elizabethan sea dogs battling with Spanish dons that we forget that the French were the enemy throughout the first part of the reign, and that Philip remained friendly for a long time.

Ever since the Middle Ages, English kings had kept up a formal claim to the French crown, which in practice worried nobody. Now, however, the position was reversed, and the claim worried Elizabeth considerably. Her cousin, Mary Queen of Scots, was married to the Dauphin of France, and became Queen of that country eight months after Elizabeth succeeded to the throne of England. But all good Catholics, Mary among them, still refused to recognize the marriage of Henry VIII and Anne Boleyn as lawful. It followed from this view that their child, Elizabeth, was debarred from the very crown she now wore. The next in succession—though Elizabeth was reluctant to admit it—was Mary.

It was a highly uncomfortable situation, full of dangerous possibilities.

Elizabeth and Cecil racked their brains over it. The war with France, which her sister had blundered into to please her husband Philip, must be wound up with as much dignity and as little loss as possible. "Calais" was certainly not written on Elizabeth's heart. She felt pretty sure the town was lost forever, and that it was not nearly so serious a loss as many people supposed. But she dared not let it go too easily. It would have upset those of her Council, and others outside, who seemed to imagine that they were still living in the age of Henry V. A treaty was therefore signed by which Calais remained an English possession in the temporary custody of France. By the time the die-hards in her Council realized that Calais had gone forever, they would probably have other things to worry about.

"The Queen poor; the realm exhausted . . . all things dear . . ."

Elizabeth's keen interest in money—some call it meanness—is one of the most famous traits in her character. Did she not take shares in some of her subjects' trading enterprises to the ends of the earth? Was she not always ready, unofficially, to claim a large part of the profits from some venture to the Spanish Main which verged on piracy, while at the same time, as Queen of England, she was blandly denying knowledge of responsibility? And did she not begrudge the cost of every cannon ball required to sink the Armada?

True, but she had her reasons. She was no miser by nature; she enjoyed life. Though her own taste in food and drink was simple, she had nothing against banquets for other people. Pageants and shows, plays and masques of all kinds she patronized. She rejoiced in fine clothes and jewels—these things were necessary to keep up her state, in an age when ambassadors and courtiers judged by appearance. Their cost was trivial compared with that of fleets and armies.

Money had worried every prince in Europe since the Spanish conquests in Mexico and South America, half a century before, had thrown vast quantities of fresh gold and silver into the markets of the Old World. As the value of those metals slumped, prices soared. In 1500, when the news of Columbus's discovery was still hot and its economic results as yet unfelt, five English pounds had bought six oxen. By Elizabeth's birth, in 1533, the same money bought little more than three. In the first years of her reign the value had fallen to slightly more than a single beast. By the end of her reign five pounds sterling would not buy an ox at all.

It was the same with most other commodities, and the same on the Continent. Elizabeth's difficulty was that, as Queen, she still had to run the country out of her own income, and much of that income, being in rents from royal lands, was fixed. Expenses went up, but revenue did not rise enough to keep pace with them. There were taxes, true, though nothing to compare with the steady, year-by-year taxation of today. They had to be voted by Parliament, which was not in daily session as nowadays, but assembled only when called. Once called together, it was apt to start interfering with other matters which she preferred to keep in her own hands. So she tried every other means she could think of, both to make money and to save it, rather than ask her "faithful Commons" for new supplies.

Her grandfather, Henry VII, had left England in a healthy financial position. Henry VIII came to the throne just as the new American gold and silver began to flood into Europe and upset the markets. Add to this the personal extravagance of that king and the years of weak, drifting government under Edward and Mary; add that the closing of the monasteries, while bringing wealth to certain families, had brought poverty and unemployment to many more; add the new boom in sheep farming (woolen cloth being now England's basic manufacture) which was good for sheep farmers and shepherds but meant starvation for plowmen and many other farm laborers; add, finally, that all her predecessors had tried to make their money stretch farther by debasing the coinage (that is, mixing too much base metal in it) so that money was no longer accepted at its face value. It will be seen then why Elizabeth's passion for economy became a byword with her courtiers.

And, to a remarkable extent, it was rewarded.

The rise in world prices was something she could not stop. With a few temporary halts and falls, it has continued ever since. But what could be done, she did.

She stopped the debasement of the coinage and reminted the money, uniform in weight and value, though she could not afford to put it back to the original standard.

Her Poor Law was a first historic move toward

our modern view that if a man cannot find work through no fault of his own, the state cannot let him starve to death.

If he cannot find work . . . But there was nothing soft and pampering about Elizabeth's charity. With Cecil's help, she sought new ways of giving the unemployed a chance to work. Foreign craftsmen were brought in to teach new trades to Englishmen. Germans came, with skill in casting cannon and mixing gunpowder, and French and Dutch Protestants, refugees from religious persecution, started the manufacture of pottery, silk, lace, and the finer qualities of cloth. As the years passed, unemployment fell and labor was even in demand. In 1563, Parliament passed the Act of Apprentices, which said that unless a man could prove that he was in a definite trade he could be directed to farmwork. Unemployment might return—it did—but it was never so bad again.

Often economy made Elizabeth take dangerous chances. When war threatened she was apt to arm late and too little. When danger passed, she demobilized—as it seemed to her commanders—too soon. Sitting there in her Privy Chamber going over accounts with the Lord Treasurer, she could not bear to think of all those men eating their heads off in camps and harbors with nothing to do. She was at one great disadvantage, compared with other monarchs: *their* troops were paid late, if ever; hers were paid regularly or sent home.

So, year by year, Elizabeth won confidence in her credit, both with the foreign bankers of Antwerp and with the Englishmen who shouldered pike or musket in her defense. England rose by degrees from bankruptcy to that prosperity and greatness which remain as a legend today.

Meanwhile, besides being a diplomat, statesman, and financial expert, Elizabeth was a warm, breathing, youthful woman, with humor and affection, jealousy and vanity, a bundle of most feminine qualities, good and bad.

Somehow she had reached the throne, at the age of twenty-five, without being married. Now that she was free to choose for herself, it was assumed that she would marry—but whom? A foreign prince? That might be almost as unpopular as Mary's marriage to Philip, and there would be fresh religious difficulties. One of her own subjects? That would make for jealousy among the nobles, however much the common people preferred an Englishman.

Elizabeth, as usual, played a waiting game. Royal marriages took much arranging. It was hard for prospective partners to meet in person: travel was so slow and difficult that she never saw the northern half of her own country, never even set eyes on Drake's Devon and Plymouth Hoe, much less any of the foreign places, Venice and Paris and Elsinore, of which Shakespeare was soon to write so glibly. Nor would royal suitors hurry to England until, like Philip in the case of Mary, they were sure to be accepted.

Photography was unknown, paintings were apt to flatter. Henry VIII's disappointment on first seeing

Anne of Cleves was a warning to his daughter. The usual practice was to call for frank confidential reports from ambassadors, doctors, and individuals sent on purpose to spy upon the character and habits of the person under consideration. When, in 1565, there was talk of Elizabeth's marrying the Archduke Charles of Austria, the Emperor's ambasador sent a hasty warning: "From now on great attention must be paid to the dress of His Princely Highness, and he should no longer make use of hacks or palfreys, but of fiery steeds . . . so that should anyone come unawares from the Queen—and this might happen very soon—he would be able to see all this."

Her Council were continually badgering her to choose a husband. Parliament moved petitions on the subject when they met; that was one reason why she summoned Parliament as rarely as she could. Until she had an heir, there would always be doubt and danger, especially since, till then, the next in line was Mary Queen of Scots.

But Elizabeth went on with her waiting game, always apparently willing to discuss the matter and drop a little encouragement here or there, as it suited her, but never coming to the point. Her Council saw the danger in delay, she saw the danger in deciding. So long as she kept all her suitors dangling, all the countries concerned were friendly to England, but, once her choice was made, the rejected countries might become her enemies. At one time or another she had ten foreign suitors for her hand. Playing them off against each other was a cheaper defense for England than fleets and armies.

Perhaps, too, there was another fear haunting the back of her mind.

Suppose, like her sister, she found herself with a foreign husband but still no children? Mary's disappointment was fresh in her memory. Some historians believe that Elizabeth felt certain she would never have children and so never meant to marry, and that all her maneuvers were just so much play-acting. We can hardly be sure now what, exactly, she knew or felt; but she must often have pondered what happened in Mary's case.

Cold she was not, for certain. She might tell the Emperor's ambassador that, left to her own private choice, she would be "beggarwoman and single, far rather than Queen and married!" That was natural pride and independence. So too, on a quite different occasion, she told a Parliamentary deputation: "I thank God that I am endued with such qualities that, if I were turned out of the realm in my petticoat, I were able to live in any place in Christendom!" So might any modern girl speak, and, the mood over, announce her engagement the following day.

But the girl who had romped with Thomas Seymour was still alive, under the robes of the Queen. When Robert Dudley (who was for a long time fancied as an English husband for her) knelt at her feet to be made Earl of Leicester, she could not resist the temptation to tickle his neck in the middle of the ceremony. Her playfulness was continually breaking out, right up to her last years—in jokes and nicknames and little human, impulsive gestures. We need not believe all the gossip which went round, some of it just innocent and ignorant exaggeration, some of it propaganda invented by her enemies; but there can be no doubt that Elizabeth was warm and affectionate, and enjoyed the friendship of men—the younger and handsomer, the better.

Robert Dudley was perhaps the man she could most happily have married. He was of her own age, had known her from childhood, and had sold some of his lands to help her when she was in disfavor during Mary's reign. He was a fine-looking young man and the perfect courtier.

Unfortunately, when only seventeen, he had married Amy Robsart. They had had no children and lived apart, she at Cumnor Place, a country house near Oxford, and he at court, where Elizabeth had appointed him to the important office of Master of the Horse.

A good deal of scandal was talked about the friendship between Elizabeth and Robert. Scandal spreads quickly in a royal household, especially if the sovereign is a young woman and unmarried. It was even rumored that Robert was planning to poison his wife, so that he could be free to marry the Queen.

Then, one September Sunday afternoon in 1560, Amy was found dead, with her neck broken, at the foot of a staircase in her country house. No one saw her die. All the servants had been given a holiday. The mystery of her death has never been cleared up completely. The jury said "accidental death," but it was probably suicide. Her husband, of course, was himself far away from the scene, but all over England—and abroad—there were supicious murmurings. It may well be that he had made Amy unhappy by his attentions to the Queen, and that Elizabeth should have kept him at a greater distance, but they can hardly be held responsible for the poor woman's death. In Tudor England, however, when all news passed from mouth to mouth, it was not easy to catch up with gossip and correct it.

Most people wished to see Robert disgraced and sent from court, but Elizabeth would not be disloyal to her friend, even though it meant sharing some of his temporary unpopularity. He was innocent, she vowed, and no one, presumably, was in a better position to know than she was herself. So he remained at court, and in due course became Earl of Leicester. But, though he was now free to remarry, Elizabeth was the one person who dared not give him her hand.

Whatever exactly had happened that Sunday afternoon at Cumnor, any hope of future marriage between them had died with Amy Robsart.

Meanwhile there arose the long, weary problem of the Queen of Scots.

To many people she has always seemed a far more romantic figure than her English cousin.

Mary, after all, was not only much courted: she was much married. Three times in all. One husband at least, Darnley, was prepared to commit murder for her sake. There was no doubt about the daggers which killed her Italian secretary, Riccio; doubt and mystery only come into the later murder of Darnley himself. Elizabeth's life, though hardly without incident, pales into dullness beside Mary's. From babyhood Mary was accustomed to wild escapes, sudden alarms, violence, and conspiracy. She ended her days on the scaffold, after long captivity, whereas Elizabeth plodded along the path of duty into old age. It is easy to depict Mary as the lovely victim, Elizabeth as the scheming villainess. Plenty of people did so then, and have done so since.

This picture hardly squares with the facts.

Early in Elizabeth's reign the problem was that Mary, Queen of Scots by right of birth, had become also Queen of France by marriage, so that England lay between two closely linked old enemies. But very soon, on the death of Mary's young husband, she returned to her own kingdom, and the problem changed. She was still linked with France, but her own ambitions lay now within the island of Britain. She was a devout Catholic and, as such, believed herself not merely the next heir to the English throne under Henry VIII's will, but its present rightful occupant instead of Elizabeth, the child of Anne Boleyn.

It was lucky for Elizabeth that Mary had not a united Scotland behind her. Instead, she was in continual struggle with her own subjects, who were more extreme in their Protestant views than the

English. After some years Mary's behavior—both personal and political—stirred them to such revolt that she had to make the last of her successful escapes. In fear of her life, not daring to wait for a ship to France, she fled across the border into England and threw herself on Elizabeth's mercy.

Elizabeth found herself in a difficult situation. If she had really wanted Mary out of the way forever, she could have sent her back to Scotland where the rebels would have dealt with her. As Mary's heir was a baby boy,* who was being brought up as a Protestant anyhow, there would have been no further trouble from that quarter.

Elizabeth would not consider such a thing. She was merciful by nature. The signing of a death warrant always caused her long hesitations and mental anguish, even when the prisoner was a man and a proved traitor. Mary was not merely a woman and her cousin, she was a queen. Elizabeth had a keen sense of rank. Subjects must *not* be allowed to punish their own sovereigns, however much they deserved it. Such a thing was unheard of. . . . And unheard of it remained, for nearly a century was still to pass before Mary's grandson, Charles I, was to be tried and executed by the Commonwealth of England.

Mary could not be sent back to Scotland, nor could she safely be sent on her way to France. She was too dangerous. No, she must remain in England, staying in a series of castles and country mansions —in appearance, an honored guest; in fact, a well-

* Later James I of England.

watched prisoner. Elizabeth did not like the arrangement, but it seemed the only one possible.

It was in 1568 that Mary fled to England. The next year came the Rising in the North—a revolt in the counties where the old religion was still strong and where Elizabeth was no more than a name. Several thousand armed men marched down into the Midlands, to rescue Mary from Tutbury Castle and make her Queen of England. But her captors whisked her away, farther south, to Coventry, and after some sharp fighting the rebels were defeated.

There was no doubt that Mary had been mixed up in the affair. Earlier in the year she had sent a message to the Spanish ambasador: "Tell the ambassador that, if his master will help me, I shall be Queen of England in three months, and Mass shall be said all over the country." But still Elizabeth took no action against her dangerous cousin, except to tighten her precautions.

In 1570 the Pope formally excommunicated Elizabeth. It was like a declaration of war. It was an open invitation to treat her not as a lawful sovereign but as a heretic usurper.

The first fruit of this was the Ridolfi plot, hatched by an Italian banker of that name in London, together with the Spanish ambassador and Mary's leading supporters. The Duke of Alva was to land six thousand Spanish troops at an English port, either Portsmouth or Harwich. They were to bring arms and money for the Englishmen who would then rise and support them. Mary was to be rescued, Elizabeth arrested. The Duke of Norfolk, on parole since his suspected share in the northern rising, was to lead the revolution and probably become Mary's fourth husband.

Cecil discovered the plot in time. Elizabeth's counterespionage department was remarkably good, considering how little money it was allowed. It was in her reign that the British Secret Service can be said to have originated.

Ridolfi crossed to the Netherlands to consult with the Duke of Alva, the Spanish commander there. Thanks to Cecil's agents abroad, one of Ridolfi's messengers was identified and arrested as he landed at Dover. The papers found on him did not reveal enough, so a spy was set on him in prison, and he was encouraged to smuggle out messages in cipher, which went straight to Cecil. Leading conspirators were referred to only by numbers, and it was some time before Cecil could break the cipher, discover that one of these numbers stood for the Duke of Norfolk, and expose the whole plot.

Norfolk was sentenced to death for high treason, but it was only after hesitating for months, and canceling several death warrants, that Elizabeth unwillingly sent him to the scaffold. She still refused to touch Mary, though Council, Parliament, and foreign governments begged her to do so and remove the danger once for all. In the whole miserable affair Elizabeth probably knew only a few minutes of grim but genuine satisfaction—when the Spanish ambassador was called in front of the

Council, told that the Queen could no longer bear his presence in the country, and ordered to get out at once.

But the plots continued. The strife, open and underground, between Catholic and anti-Catholic became more and more bitter throughout Europe. Soon after the Ridolfi plot at home, Elizabeth was shocked—and England almost maddened—by the Massacre of St. Bartholomew, in which thousands of Protestants, men, women, and children, were murdered in Paris and other French cities. A few years later English Jesuit Fathers* began to re-enter England in disguise, and while to followers of the old religion they came as heroic missionaries, to Elizabeth and the rest of her people they seemed the secret agents of an enemy power. For the first seventeen years of her reign she had been able to boast that no man had been executed for his religion. Now that religion and politics had become so hopelessly entwined, she could keep that record no longer. If a man, either Catholic or extreme Puritan, was guilty of treason, he paid the penalty. No doubt there were some innocent victims. The courts were far from perfect, and frightened men make harsh judges, but throughout the rest of her long reign the number of these executions did not amount to more than two-thirds of the number in her sister's five or six years.

At last, though, the Queen of Scots could no longer be spared. She had gone on plotting. Letters passed by many ingenious means—sometimes in a

* Members of the Society of Jesus, founded in 1540.

waterproof case inside a barrel of beer—but Elizabeth's Secret Service was watchful. "You have much secret communication with the Queen of Scotland," said Elizabeth to the French ambassador, looking him straight in the eye, "but believe me, I know all that goes on in my kingdom. I was a prisoner myself, in the time of the Queen, my sister. I know the tricks that prisoners use to bribe servants and get secret information."

She did. A plot to kill her was made by a young gentleman named Babington. One of Mary's letters to him, approving the plan and making suggestions, went straight into the waiting hands of the Secret Service. Mary was arrested, tried, and sentenced to death. Elizabeth hesitated to the end. Early in November of 1587 both Houses of Parliament voted unanimously for the sentence to be carried out; they renewed the demand three weeks later, but it was not till the first of February that she signed the warrant. Just one week afterward, Mary's nineteen years of captivity ended on a black-draped scaffold in the great hall of Fotheringay Castle. Patriotic Londoners celebrated with bonfires and feastings, but Elizabeth herself was so unhappy that she could neither eat nor sleep.

With Mary dead, nothing short of a foreign invasion at full strength could shake her from the throne. Next year the attempt was made. It was 1588, the year of the Armada.

"Good captains and soldiers wanting," the Council had lamented when Elizabeth came to the

throne. Now, thirty years later, it was a different story.

So far as possible she had kept the peace—but it had been hard to stop adventurous gentlemen wandering overseas on their own account, and she had a knack of smiling while she looked the other way.

In 1580 she had gone aboard *The Golden Hind* to knight Francis Drake when he returned from his three-year voyage round the world. In that trip he had sacked the Spanish colony of Valparaiso, seized the yearly treasure convoy from Peru, and explored the North Pacific coast as far as where San Francisco stands today. He had formally "occupied" that unknown territory in the Queen's name as New Albion, even before Raleigh had first tried to colonize Virginia.

Drake was only the foremost of such captains. There were Hawkins, Grenville, Humphrey Gilbert, Frobisher, and many more. They were not all very virtuous characters—some dabbled in slave trading and piracy—but when Elizabeth needed fighting men she could have wished for no better material.

So, too, with her soldiers. While Drake and his sort were on the Spanish Main, others were learning their trade on land—helping the Huguenots as volunteers in France, fighting the Spaniards in the Netherlands, or trying to conquer Ireland. The most famous of these gentlemen-adventurers, Sir Philip Sidney, did not come back alive, but many others did. If the Spaniards had ever disembarked in England, they would have met with a warm welcome.

It is easy for modern historians to explain to us that the Armada was never so dangerous as it seemed at the time. We know now that it comprised only about the same number of ships as the English force against it; that the Spanish galleons were not really larger than the English vessels, but of about the same tonnage, only differently designed; that they were slower, less skillfully handled, and overcrowded with troops; and that their guns were fewer, lighter, and of shorter range.

Henry VIII had laid the foundations of the English victory half a century before. It was owing to his interest in gunnery and ship design that the porthole had been invented, allowing heavier cannon to be fitted and fired from a level closer to the water line.

Drake and his friends were confident enough. Unlike the general public, they knew the facts. They knew they could smash the Armada if they met it. The danger was, in that age of sail, that they might miss it. Then, if the Spanish troops got ashore, it might be a different matter. On land, the Spaniard was the best fighting man in Europe. And the defending forces were naturally scattered throughout England, since it was not known where the invasion might be made. There were coastal defenses right from Land's End to the Wash, halfway up the eastern side of the kingdom.

The most probable landing place, however, was the southeastern corner, where the Duke of Parma's forces, waiting in the Netherlands, would have only a narrow strip of sea to cross, and then a short distance to march on London. Elizabeth's main army was therefore gathered at Tilbury, on the northern bank of the Thames, just where it widens toward the open sea. Their commander was that same Earl of Leicester, still her friend, whom she loved, probably, more than any other man she had ever known.

This was the moment when Elizabeth showed the full glory of her character. She took coach to Tilbury, and then, mounting a great white horse and holding a marshal's baton, rode through the dense ranks of her army, heedless of the danger from traitors. Her speech to the troops is quoted in every book about her, but it is impossible not to quote it again, because those ringing words so vividly bring her to life again before our eyes.

"My loving people," she said, "we have been persuaded by some that are careful of our safety, to take heed how we commit ourselves to armed multitudes, for fear of treachery. But I assure you, I do not desire to live to distrust my faithful and loving people. Let tyrants fear. I have always so behaved myself that, under God, I have placed my chiefest strength and safeguard in the loyal hearts and good will of my subjects; and therefore I am come amongst you, as you see, at this time, not for my recreation and disport, but being resolved, in the midst and heat of the battle, to live or die amongst you all—to lay down for my God, and for my kingdom, and for my people, my honour and my blood, even in the dust. I know I have the body of a weak and feeble woman, but I have the heart and stomach of a king, and of a king of England too, and think foul scorn that Parma or Spain, or any prince of Europe should dare to invade the borders of my realm. . . ."

That was not only Elizabeth at her finest, but Elizabethan prose at its best—which was very good indeed, second only to Elizabethan poetry.

Everyone knows how the Armada was destroyed at sea, so that the Tilbury soldiers never needed to fire a shot. In the midst of the national rejoicings the Queen suffered a great personal loss. The Earl of Leicester died of a fever. He had written a letter to Elizabeth a week before, and the news of his death followed hard on its delivery. We know that she wrote on the paper *"his last letter,"* and perhaps those three words tell us as much about her private feelings as we are ever likely to discover.

Leicester was followed as Master of the Horse and also as intimate friend by another, younger Robert—Robert Devereux, Earl of Essex. He had been in the host at Tilbury, with his own company of horsemen and musketeers, gaily uniformed in orange with white silk facings.

Essex was barely twenty-one, a handsome, brilliant, swaggering boy. Elizabeth was fifty-five, healthy, strong, and vigorous, as indeed she remained until the end, but painfully conscious that her looks were fading. She had had smallpox years before. She relied more and more, now, on the crude make-up of that century, and even on false hair. As a Queen she remained magnificent: as a human being she began to deserve pity as well as admiration.

It was natural that she should be attracted to the Earl of Essex—that she should treat him sometimes like a son, sometimes like a lover. The exaggerated language of the court, the flattering phrases which everyone was expected to use to the sovereign, made a relationship normal to them which might sound ridiculous to our own ears. And there is little doubt that Essex, in his mounting pride and ambition, would cheerfully have married this aging woman if he could have sat beside her as King of England.

Without this friendship, Elizabeth would have been lonely indeed. Leicester was dead. Raleigh, once her pet, had infuriated her by getting married, and was banished from court. Cecil was growing very old, and was handing over more and more of his work to his cold-blooded, efficient, but unattractive son. The old man survived for ten years after the Armada, and Elizabeth never showed herself more human than when she went to see him on his sickbed, and fed him with her own hand. She had told him, once, that she had no wish to live on, herself, after she lost him. But she had no choice.

So it was Essex who dominated the last years of the century—Essex dancing, jesting, quarreling with the Queen, leading expeditions against Cádiz and the Spanish treasure fleet, fighting campaigns against the Irish, acting as patron to Shakespeare and Bacon and other rising authors of the day.

It seemed that Elizabeth doted on him. But there was something in her character which always halted her before she could make a fool of herself. Thoughts of marriage and children were distant memories. Her affection for Essex may have gone far beyond the airy compliments of court conversation, but it did not reach a consuming passion.

There came a moment when Essex realized that he had risen as high as he could. Elizabeth would never share the throne of England with him. Frenzied with ambition and conceit, counting on his own popularity and a certain discontent which troubled the country in her declining years, he headed the last of the many conspiracies against her.

She was sitting at dinner in her palace at Whitehall when the news was brought that Essex was marching through the London streets, collecting arms and men. She refused to seek safety.

"He who placed me on this throne," she said, "will preserve me on it."

"She would have gone out in person," reported an eyewitness later, "to see what any rebel of them all durst do against her, had not her councilors with much ado stayed her." This was the winter of 1601. She was by then sixty-seven, a really old woman for those days, the oldest monarch in Europe. Yet her calm courage did much to save the situation, for the actual troops at her disposal were few.

The revolt collapsed. Essex was condemned to death and beheaded. This time Elizabeth did not hesitate over signing the warrant. Essex was senseless and ungrateful, she said; he "had at last revealed what had long been in his mind." Many women of her age might have been spiteful and savage, feeling that they had been made to look foolish by a young man's flattery. Elizabeth had her feelings, as always, under control. Essex and five ringleaders had to pay the penalty, the other rebels were let off with light punishments or none at all.

The Queen turned back to her sheaves of state papers. England had still to be governed. But now, more than ever, she must have felt alone.

Elizabeth herself was withering like some ancient, splendid tree. But the Elizabethan Age, as future generations were to call it, was still putting out its finest blossoms.

Shakespeare was writing *Hamlet, Julius Caesar,* and *Twelfth Night.* Ben Jonson and several of the other playwrights were beginning to produce their first mature work. Bacon's *Essays* were newly published in their first edition, and Hakluyt's *Voyages* had come out in a much enlarged one.

Nor were Englishmen voyaging only in print. The year 1600 saw the foundation of the East India Company, which led in time to the British rule over India. Other traders and explorers were venturing into every quarter of the globe—Turkey, Russia, Africa, the Spanish Main. One, William Adams, even rounded Cape Horn and went to Japan, where he settled with a Japanese wife and taught the people to build their first navy. Like the ancient Athenians, Elizabeth's subjects could have boasted, "we have forced every sea and land to be the highway of our daring. . . ."

At home, meanwhile, there had been many changes. Life was more comfortable, and, except for noblemen who meddled in treason, more secure. In his *Description of England,* published just before the Armada year, a clergyman named William Harrison had written how great had been the improvements in living memory. New farmhouses and cottages dotted the countryside. Their brick chimneys were one symbol of the age: it was not so long since the poorer people had made do with a hole in the roof. Sheets and feather beds had replaced the prickly straw and canvas mattresses. Furniture, food, and clothing were better for most people. Outside, new flowers and fruits and trees, introduced from far-off lands by men such as Raleigh, brought the New World into the gardens which were becoming a passion with Englishmen, as they have remained to the present day.

Such was the inheritance she bequeathed to James Stuart and the seventeenth century. She fell ill in March, 1603, but would neither go to bed nor take medicine. She had outlived her friends, she was old and tired and lonely, and she knew that not only James, but many of her own councilors, were waiting for her to die. She herself felt no desire to stay. She sent for Archbishop Whitgift, whom in happier hours she had jokingly nicknamed her "black husband," and he helped her to prepare for death.

In the early hours of March 24, before dawn, she who had never seen more than half of her earthly kingdom glided peacefully away into a new one of which none of her captains, neither Drake nor Raleigh nor Humphrey Gilbert, had ever brought back word.

THE YEARS BETWEEN

1603–1662

Elizabeth was succeeded by her cousin, James VI of Scotland, who became James I of England and founded the Stuart line. This was the century of struggle between Crown and Parliament. Elizabeth had usually managed to control Parliament in her own highhanded way, but the new Scottish kings, James I and Charles I, were less popular. They were as self-willed as she had been, but they lacked her charm and humor. Also, as England grew in prosperity, the new middle class of merchants, lawyers, and country squires (the smaller landowners), realized their power and demanded a say in the government. Two parties were formed, the Royalists (or Cavaliers) and the Parliamentarians (or Roundheads—a sneering nickname which referred to their shorter haircuts), and a civil war was fought. It ended in victory for Parliament under Oliver Cromwell and the beheading of King

Charles. His sons, afterward Charles II and James II, escaped abroad. Cromwell's victory did not, however, bring in democracy. He was forced by circumstances to set up a military dictatorship with himself as Lord Protector, England being a kind of republic termed "the Commonwealth." This system collapsed soon after his death, and 1660 saw the "Restoration" of the Stuart kings. Charles II came back from Holland and was crowned. With him came his brother James, Duke of York, who became the father, a year or two later, of the two little girls destined to reign as Mary II and Anne. Life under the Protectorate had been somewhat grim and puritanical. The theaters had been closed, Christmas festivities forbidden, and sport discouraged. For this reason the Restoration brought a violent swing in the opposite direction, so that lighthearted gaiety degenerated, in high society, into evil living.

ŌŌŌŌ

MARY—AND WILLIAM

After Elizabeth, nearly a century was to pass before another woman came to the throne of England—a century as full of drama as the one which had preceded it. Elizabeth I closes the sixteenth, the Tudor century. Mary II almost ends the seventeenth, or Stuart, century. For, though strictly speaking one more Stuart is to follow, her younger sister Anne, most of us see Anne as an eighteenth-century figure, paired with the Duke of Marlborough against the smoky background of Blenheim and the other great victories over France. It is Mary who, though only slightly older in years, belongs to the age of Cavaliers and Roundheads, whose struggles provide the chief theme of seventeenth-century English history.

No reigning queen of England is so little remembered as this Mary is today. There is not even a a picturesque story tagged to her, like that escape across the frozen river which keeps the name of Maud alive in modern memory. "William and Mary. . . ." If spoken of at all, she is always bracketed with her famous husband, William of Orange. Their joint names are applied to a certain period in antique furniture and house architecture, and to a few institutions she endowed, such as the William and Mary College in Virginia. Was she really such a complete nonentity, just the wife of her husband —or was she a person in her own right, just as she was in her own right a queen?

The story of Mary is well worth tracking through the records of the period.

She was born, then, on April 30, 1662, at St. James's Palace in London. The building itself looked very much as it does today—and did when Elizabeth II was proclaimed from its balcony. It is still, in name, the seat of the royal court, and foreign ambassadors are still accredited "to the Court of St. James's." But just as the larger Buckingham Palace is the London home of the present Queen, so, when Mary was born, her uncle Charles II lived in Whitehall Palace, a short walk across the park, and had given St. James's to his younger brother James, Duke of York, to live in.

All this corner of modern London is full of memories of that time. Charles loved St. James's park, and was already hard at work beautifying it when his niece was born. It was he who had the broad avenue laid down which is now the Mall, the processional way down which later sovereigns have driven from Buckingham Palace to their weddings and coronations. And he, too, who established the aviaries which are recalled in the name Birdcage Walk. Mary's childhood memories must have included the sight of her gay, easygoing uncle strolling across the park with a little crowd of toy spaniels frothing at his heels.

She was born in the first lighthearted, almost hysterical days of the Restoration, which brought the Stuarts back to the throne.

It had not been four years since the death of Oliver Cromwell, and just two years since the King and her parents had returned from years of poverty-stricken exile beyond the seas. Roundhead rule was dead. Once more it was legal to have music in church, to go to the theater or the horse races, to keep Christmas with all the good old customs, to dance round the Maypole at the coming of spring. On the surface England was a happier, freer country. Only as the glamor of the Restoration wore off did people realize that none of the deeper problems had been solved by the mere return of the King, especially such a king as Charles. It may be noted in passing that during his reign more and more of his subjects preferred the hardships of the new American colonies to all the attractions of "good King Charles's golden days." North and South Carolina were both founded at this time, and Pennsylvania toward his latter years, while New York, New Jersey, and Delaware, taken from the Dutch when Mary was in the nursery, soon attracted their share of Englishmen and Scots. It was not only the persecuted Puritans who emigrated; there were Royalists too, who had expected too much of the new government and had been bitterly disappointed.

Mary's father, the future James II, was a tall, gloomy-featured, haughty young man—he had been born in that same palace twenty-eight years before. He was narrow-minded and obstinate, as immoral in his private life as Charles, but without any of that charm and humor which made many people forgive the elder brother his weaknesses. He did good work for the Navy, for he was an efficient organizer though almost overstrict in his discipline. If he could have stayed at the Admiralty instead of succeeding to the throne, he might have left a more popular memory.

Mary's mother was Anne Hyde, who, like Anne Boleyn, came of an ordinary English family, though her lawyer father, thanks to his abilities and his loyalty to Charles in exile, had been made Lord Chancellor and Earl of Clarendon. She was a quiet, undistinguished young woman, without any striking beauty of face, though she had fine hands and arms and a figure which, while attractive at first in a plump way, soon ran to excessive fat. Indeed, the Duchess of York quite frankly overate, and did her best to pass on the bad habit to her children. Anne especially, Mary's younger sister, was encouraged "to sup with her on chocolate and devour good things, till she grew as round as a ball," and was made so ill that she had to be sent away for a holiday.

Mary, like many princesses before her, caused disappointment when she was born. "I find nobody pleased," Pepys wrote in his secret diary. The King had no children. It already seemed likely that the crown would pass to the Duke of York and his. Still, there was ample time for sons. There were formal rejoicings for Mary, and she was baptized with Prince Rupert as godfather—the once dashing cavalry general of the Civil War, who had since turned his mind to naval matters, science, and the Hudson's Bay Company. A year or two later Pepys noted how he came upon the Duke playing "with his little girl just like an ordinary private father of a child," so he had evidently recovered from his disappointment and was not as coldhearted as he usually seemed.

But Stuart princesses, like Tudors, were not in close daily touch with their parents. There was an unsettled period when Mary was three and Anne a mere baby. The plague raged in London all through the summer and autumn of 1665 and the court fled from the city. Charles went to Oxford, James and his family to York. It seemed better for the King and his heirs to be apart, lest the infection should strike down the whole royal family at a blow. The following year saw the Fire of London, which, though it did not reach nearly to Whitehall or St. James's, left the old city in ruins. And a year later, with reconstruction just under way, it looked as though a Dutch fleet might sweep right up the Thames. Mary was still only five, but already her tiny lifetime had spanned a good deal of history. It was small wonder that she and her sister were kept away from these perils, and given a household of their own, under Lady Frances Villiers, at Richmond Palace, a few miles farther up the winding river.

It must have been a pleasant place to live in. Richmond was a splendid Tudor palace, rising from the bank like a cliff with a skyline of soaring pinnacles. It was set in the great park which is still a favorite resort of modern Londoners, and had its own spacious gardens and orchards. Nor was it lonely, for Lady Villiers had six girls and a boy of her own, and there were other children, including Mary's bosom friend, Frances Apsley, some of whom shared lessons with the small Princesses. There was a whole staff of masters and tutors, so that the place was not unlike a highly select boarding school.

Drawing was taught by two dwarfs, Mr. and Mrs. Gibson, neither of whom was more than three and a half feet tall. They had met and married at the court of Queen Henrietta Maria—relics of a cruder age, when people saw nothing wrong in smiling at human deformity, and royal dwarfs were kept almost as pets. It is good to know that this tiny pair had a long and happy life, Mrs. Gibson living almost to a hundred, and having nine children who grew to normal size. Mr. Gibson was a good friend to Mary, and used to carry her private notes to Frances Apsley. Like many other schoolgirls since, the two friends got great pleasure from pouring out these letters to each other, even when they were meeting at frequent intervals throughout the day.

In spite of all the teachers who were available,

the education of the Princesses was a very poor thing compared with that of the Tudors. There was no discipline, and they were left to study or not as they pleased. Mary seems to have attempted no foreign language but French, which was absolutely necessary for court life, and opinions vary about her success. Not unnaturally, her French tutor, Peter de Laine, reported that she was a perfect mistress of the language. At least she spelled it no worse than she spelled her own, but that is not saying a great deal.

She was growing up in an age of fascinating intellectual activity, but she seems to have been largely unaware of it. The Royal Society had just been founded and scientific research was starting in a dozen directions. Navigators were pushing into the last of the unknown seas. In North America, in the West Indies, and in India, the British Empire was springing to life. In music and literature England was experiencing a splendid silver age, second only to the golden age of the Tudors. Isaac Newton, Christopher Wren, Halley the astronomer, Robert Boyle, "the father of chemistry," Milton, Bunyan, and a host of others were alive and at work. The royal family were not all without serious interests—the King himself and Mary's godfather Prince Rupert, for instance, dabbled in amateur science—but nobody thought it necessary that the two little Princesses should be told of what was happening in the world around them.

True, neither Mary nor Anne had the keen brain of Elizabeth, and they could not have responded as fully as she would have done. But they were not fools, and if, later in their lives, they did not always show up to the best advantage, some of the blame can fairly be laid to the lack of stimulus in their education.

Mary rode and was fond of walking. Her chief pleasure, though, seems to have been dancing. Pepys saw her "dancing most finely" when she was very small, and, as she grew older, she was taken more and more to court and allowed to take part in the masques and ballets.

She was twelve and a half when she appeared in the first of these, playing the title role in *Calisto, or the Chaste Nymph,* while Anne played the "juvenile lead," Nymphe. Sarah Jennings (afterward Duchess of Marlborough) was the god Mercury, and the ill-fated Duke of Monmouth danced in the ballet. The two Princesses had been coached by a famous actress, Mrs. Betterton, whose training helped them in later life as queens, when their speech and bearing became all-important. Dryden had written a special epilogue, addressed to the King, and referring to his nieces as:

> *"Two glorious nymphs of your own godlike line,*
> *Whose morning rays like noontide strike and shine. . . ."*

It was not just a courtier's flattery. If not quite "glorious nymphs," they were good-looking girls. Mary was a true Stuart, slim and graceful, with dark hair and eyes, good features, and a clear skin. Anne favored her mother, but that rosy chubbiness was attractive enough at the age of ten.

Their mother had died some years before, when Mary was nine, and their father had remarried. Their stepmother, Mary of Modena, was a beautiful Italian princess. We read that she "appear'd about fourteen years of age; she was tall, and admirably shaped, her complexion was of the last fairness, her hair black as jet, so were her eyebrows and her eyes; but the latter so full of light and sweetness so they did dazzle and charm too." She was, in fact, fifteen at the time of her marriage. The gap between her and her stepdaughters was so narrow that James, when introducing them to each other, could say to the younger girls: "I have provided you a playfellow."

It was a pity they could not "play" together more. The new Duchess was not only beautiful but one of the most accomplished princesses of her day, with wit, character, and an almost Tudor fluency in foreign languages. She was one of the healthier elements in a court rotten with immorality and false values.

She was, however, a Roman Catholic, as James was—and religion was still such a bitter political question that not even he, let alone this new stepmother, was allowed to influence that side of Mary's upbringing. Parliament was determined that both Princesses should be Protestants. They were free to grow up ignorant in other ways; it was quite all right for them to be plunged, as schoolgirls, into the corrupt and immoral atmosphere of Whitehall Palace; but the bishops must be able to guarantee them as sheep of the approved Church of England flock.

As it happened, Mary survived the test of her character and picked up nothing worse from court life than a passion for cardplaying, which she indulged even on Sundays until stopped. Later, when out of England, she revived this Sunday evening habit, but she coupled it with much religious reading, almost the only serious reading she undertook.

She went on with her dancing and acting. When she was fourteen she appeared in a masque as Diana, the goddess of the hunt. We have her portrait, by Sir Peter Lely, the court painter of the day, with bow and arrow, and a crescent moon upon her brow. But she was about to say good-by to girlhood. She was to be married at fifteen.

Dryden had foretold her probable future when, continuing those verses about the "two glorious nymphs," he had written, still addressing the King:

"Whom you to suppliant monarchs shall dispose
To bind your friends and to disarm your foes."

The "friend," in Mary's case, was Holland, the "foe" was France.

She was completely unprepared. She knew, of course, that her cousin,* William of Orange, was over in England on a visit to discuss state matters with her uncle, the King. But she had not the slightest idea that she herself was one of the state matters, bracketed with a proposed treaty between Eng-

* His mother, now dead, had been sister to Charles II and James.

land and the Dutch republic and a switchover from Charles's former pro-French foreign policy.

She was then in London, at St. James's. Her father came in just after noon, having dined at Whitehall. His face was grave and angry as he took Mary into her room and shut the door. Then he told her. Much against his own will—but his brother the King was forcing him—she was to marry William.

The young girl looked aghast. When, she asked?

Almost at once, said the Duke grimly. Two weeks hence, on Sunday, November 4, that being the Prince's birthday—his twenty-seventh—as well as his late mother's and the anniversary of his father's death. There was yet another coincidence of dates which no one then foresaw: eleven years hence, the Prince was to celebrate his birthday and wedding anniversary at sea off the Devon coast, on the eve of invading England and pushing his father-in-law off the throne.

Even if Mary had known this, her grief could hardly have been more passionate. She was still a child, a schoolgirl who had not even had the advantage of attending a proper school. She was still more interested in slipping sentimental little notes to her best friend than in any dealings with the opposite sex, least of all a grim general and statesman such as William. And in a few weeks she was to be carried off to a foreign country far from her sister and father, her home and her beloved Frances Apsley.

The Duke was so furious over the wedding on his

own account—he had hoped for a Catholic husband who would have won Mary to the Roman Church—that he probably did not handle the interview with much tact or sympathy.

Mary wept all that afternoon and evening. She wept on the following day when the Privy Council came to congratulate her. She was never far from tears during the succeeding days when one official deputation after another arrived to tell her, in high-flown seventeenth-century phrases, how pleased everyone felt and what a lucky girl she was.

James, still furious at being forced into this arrangement, did not pay too much heed to his daughter's red eyes. Had not Mary of Modena, at the very same age, wept rebelliously at the prospect of marrying him? Girls must not expect to choose their own husbands. But for their fathers' wishes to be overruled—that was scandalous indeed.

The bridegroom was certainly one of the most remarkable men in Europe at that time.

Though known as the Prince of Orange—a family title taken from the town of that name in Southern France—William was officially the Stadholder of the United Provinces, that is, head of the Dutch republic. This small country had, within a generation or two, become one of the leading powers in Europe. It had fought Cromwell's fleet and, later, the ill-paid navy of King Charles. On land, under the Prince's brilliant generalship, it rallied the opposition against Louis XIV of France.

To William, this marriage was just a move of

statecraft, to strengthen his position with England and administer a slap in the face to King Louis. He was not interested in Mary as a person, or in any other girl or woman. He was a hard-bitten, simple-living soldier, utterly different from his two uncles and all the other gentry who (with ladies little better than themselves) had made Whitehall the most scandalous court in English history.

All he wanted in a wife, as he himself admitted, was someone to provide a quiet home where he could find peace from the worries of generalship and government. It was not, perhaps, a very exciting ideal, but it was an improvement on that of most other princes of the age. As it turned out, it was to suit Mary well enough.

In himself, William was a presentable bridegroom. Looking at him, Mary recognized many of the familiar Stuart features—the full mouth set in the oval face, the dark reddish-brown hair, the dark almond-shaped eyes so like her own. He had never been strong, but he had toughened himself by soldiering, hunting, and riding. He was a superb horseman. He was no lady's man and had no witty small talk, but he had dignity. He was a man she could look up to, and as she grew to know him she did.

But there was no time to know him before the wedding. And it was surely one of the most miserable, unromantic royal weddings on record.

It was a private, family affair in Mary's own room at the palace. It took place at nine o'clock on a November night. Mary's feelings and her father's are well known. Her sister was out of sorts—her illness soon proved to be smallpox. William was much as usual, grave, reserved, correct, but unenthusiastic. The only happy face was that of the King, swarthy, cynically smiling, the full lips parting at intervals to make jokes which were coarse, or irreverent, or both.

The formalities were completed. The quill pens scratched in the candlelight. Mary was Princess of Orange and a married woman. She was just fifteen and a half.

William's mission to England was accomplished. His one desire was to get home, out of the unhealthy atmosphere of Whitehall and St. James's.

It was, at that moment, literally unhealthy. Mary's sister had developed smallpox, the scourge of society in that age, which had killed both William's parents and had almost killed him. Mary refused to leave Anne; William ordered her to keep out of danger. There were quarrels. William stood firm. Mary knew where she stood from that day forth. William meant to be master.

The winter had broken early. The North Sea was lashed by storms. The King warned William that, if he sailed, he might go straight to the bottom with his new wife. But on November 19, two weeks after the marriage, they left Whitehall by boat and went down the Thames to Erith, where they boarded the yacht *Mary,* one of the new fast-sailing craft which the Dutch had recently invented. William said they would go if it was possible for the vessel to make any progress at all in the teeth of the wind.

Mary of Modena tried to comfort the Princess by reminding her that she herself, at the same age, had been forced to leave her home for an unknown country. Mary had stared at her through her tears and answered, with that English smugness which either delights or infuriates other nations, according to their sense of humor:

"But, madam, *you* were coming to England—and I am leaving it!"

The weather prophets had been right and William wrong. The yacht could make no headway. They disembarked, spent several days at Canterbury (William did not really mind, he had got away from London, which was the main thing), and took another ship from Margate. The Dutch coast was sighted a day later, but, as the River Maas was choked with ice, they had to land at Teyheyden and drive for two hours through a bitter wind to William's palace at Honslaerdyke.

In normal weather the journey would have been easy. Mary was going to a foreign land but not a far-off one. In actual fact Holland could be reached from London, in those days, much more quickly than many towns in the north or west of England When, in the following autumn, her stepmother and sister were planning a visit, Mary of Modena could write in a letter to Italy: "If the wind is favorable, in twenty-four hours after leaving this house we should reach that of the Princess of Orange." There was a fair service for mail and ordinary passengers throughout Charles's reign, the Dutch vessels being considered much better than the English, and soon (from 1687 onward) there was to be an efficient regular packet service, largely due to William's efforts.

Nor could everything in Holland have struck Mary as strange and unfamiliar.

For a generation or more—despite some years of naval war—the two countries had been in close contact. People often make the mistake of thinking that all the Dutch elements in English life (architectural features, fashions in garden layout, and so on) were brought in with William and Mary in 1689. In fact, England had been taking ideas from the go-ahead little Dutch republic long before then. Dutch engineers had drained the Fens, Dutch artists painted the beauties of Charles's court, Dutch shipbuilders, metalworkers, glass and china manufacturers and weavers were engaged in English industry. When Mary looked around her at the brick houses and curly "Dutch" gables, she was only seeing something which had been more and more imitated at home in recent years.

The Holland which was to be Mary's home for the next eleven years has been kept for us in the famous pictures of Vermeer, De Hooch, Hobbema, and other artists whose work, besides being scattered through the art galleries of the world, can be seen everywhere in reproductions and book illustrations. Through the eyes of these painters we can look into the bright clean homes of Holland and their paved courtyards, see the maids preparing the food, the young mistress admiring herself in the glass or taking her music lesson, and the men at cards over their wine—and see, too, the windmills, the baggy-breeched countrymen playing skittles, the summer rivers crowded with sails, and the winter ones dotted with skaters.

Mary learned to skate, too. It was a new sport for English people in those days. It was not William who taught her, however, but her English cousin, the Duke of Monmouth, when he came on a visit. William was probably too busy.

Her new home was not the great moated palace of the Hague. That was for state assemblies, and she seldom went there. She lived, instead, about a mile away in a mansion known as the Palace in the Wood, because it was surrounded by an oak forest and approached by a superb avenue of similar trees. William had added two new wings to this palace in honor of his bride.

Life was quiet there compared with her existence in England. Amsterdam and the other busy cities were far away and the Hague was little more than a beautifully laid-out political capital, grouped round the palace of the same name. Holland was a republic of prosperous businessmen, with no court society to gather round the Prince and Princess. William himself was away much of the time with his armies. When at home, he was deep in official papers or riding out to hunt. He had the tastes of a country gentleman. He was interested in gardens and houses, not in books or music. Mary had to make her own amusements, with the English ladies she had been allowed to bring with her.

She seems to have been happy enough, once she

got used to the separation from England. She was soon deeply in love with the quiet, grave husband whom she had taken so tearfully a little while before. William, though not one to show his feelings, grew to return that love. It was only years later, when he broke down with grief at losing her, that people realized how much she had meant to him. If they had had children, their married life would have been complete.

Meanwhile, in the outside world, much was happening. While Mary strolled through the oak woods, or drove over to the potteries of Delft to see new porcelain, or toured the canals and rivers by barge, needlework on lap and her English chaplain reading aloud, events were moving to a climax.

Her uncle Charles died in 1685 and her father became king, to the great alarm of the anti-Catholics. Many would have preferred the Protestant Duke of Monmouth, even though he was not Charles's lawful son. Soon Mary had letters telling of the rising in the West Country against her father, then of his army's triumph at Sedgemoor, and finally of Monmouth's capture and execution.

Monmouth had been her cousin. It seemed such a little time since he had been here in Holland, teaching her to skate. . . . Not so many years, even, since he had danced in the ballet when she played the nymph Calisto. . . .

No doubt she shook her head sadly, and remarked—quite truthfully—that she did not know what things were coming to.

William had a shrewd idea. He had held aloof

from the Monmouth rebellion, making no false move. Give James enough rope and he would hang himself. . . .

James had no children by his second, Catholic wife. Mary was his probable successor, Anne next, and William himself third in the line. But would James—so haughty, so obstinate, and so bigoted—manage to control his Protestant subjects for the rest of his life?

During the next three years James proceeded, step by step, to unite the English people—against himself. Not only were there religious changes, but he raised a large standing army; the very idea of such a thing had been hateful to Englishmen since Cromwell had used his military power to overrule Parliament. Also, James put Irish Catholic officers into as many commands as possible, and garrisoned the troops just outside London as an open warning to the citizens.

Each new move was quickly reported to William. Fast yachts were constantly flitting across the North Sea, carrying dispatches in code, and, as time passed, appeals signed by leading Englishmen that William should come to the rescue.

The last straw was the birth of a son to Mary of Modena. Automatically this baby became heir to the throne, displacing his half sister Mary. Politically, his birth came at the most convenient moment for James—so convenient, indeed, that many people would not believe he was really the King and Queen's child, but a newborn male baby who had been smuggled into the palace from outside. Both

Mary and Anne were led to believe in this supposed plot, and were deeply indignant over what they considered to be their father's wickedness.

His motive seemed obvious. All these years it had grown more and more probable that the crown would fall, at James's death, into the Protestant hands of the Princess of Orange. So, to those who disliked James's policy, it had been just a question of waiting patiently. Time was on their side. But now all was altered. Time had changed sides. They must act now or never, before a new line of Catholic kings was firmly established on the throne.

William saw it as a European problem. He was not personally ambitious to control England. His eyes were always on wider, Continental horizons. But, for that very reason, he needed a friendly Protestant England at his back. He dared not let the island join his enemies.

To Mary it was more of a religious question. She did not understand politics. She had never been trained to, as a girl, and William had never wished to explain them. When he was with her, his one desire was to forget the worries of state business. But the one thing which had been thoroughly drummed into Mary by bishops and chaplains from her earliest youth was the rightness of her own religion and the scheming wickedness of people who held other beliefs.

It was not easy to turn against her own father. It was made possible only by two things: her religious faith, which was as fanatical as his own but opposed to it; and her passionate love for her husband, which overcame her natural affections as a daughter.

She clutched at the story of the false baby. If she could make herself believe that her father had done that, it would satisfy her conscience. It would make everything that William meant to do seem so right and necessary!

How much did she actually know at the time, when William was receiving those appeals from England and mustering ships and men for the expedition? William, after all, was continually busy with warlike preparations against somebody. . . . But certainly she must have known and guessed more than she revealed in her letters home. Good, simple soul though she was, Mary would lie—or at least avoid telling the whole truth—if it helped her beloved husband.

On September 28, 1688, her stepmother wrote to her from Whitehall:

"I am put to it what to say, at a time when nothing is talked of here but the Prince of Orange coming over with an army. This has been said a long time and believed by a great many, but I do protest to you I never did believe it till now very lately, that I have no possibility left of doubting it. The second part of this news I will never believe, that is that you are to come over with him; for I know you to be too good, that I don't believe you could have such a thought against the worst of fathers, much less perform it against the best, that has always been kind to you, and I believe has loved you better than all the rest of his children."

The final phrase refers to the other children who, apart from Anne, had all died young.

James himself wrote by the same post, saying that he hoped William's plan "will have been as great a surprise to you as it was to me, when I first heard it, being sure it is not in your nature to approve of so unjust an undertaking."

Mary, however, saw nothing unjust in it. She hardened her heart. After the events of that autumn she cut herself off from James entirely. They neither saw each other again nor corresponded.

The Glorious Revolution, which finally drove James from the throne, belongs more to the story of Anne, who lived through it in England, than to that of Mary, who passed those anxious weeks at the Palace in the Wood. Mary has left a brief journal covering each year of her life at this period. In it she describes the anguish of her farewell to William, when he set off on the desperate adventure from which he might never return:

"After the dinner I accompanied him to the bank of the river. . . . It was there that I saw him for the last time and God alone knows if we shall ever see one another again. This thought was so terrible that it deprived me for some time of my senses, for I remained without movement in my carriage and had not the power to tell them to go on as long as I could see the Prince."

Then came the anxious waiting for news, and that, when it came, came not from William himself but from London. He had landed at Torbay, in the far west, on November 5, and unfurled his banner with its legend, *"I will maintain the Protestant religion and the liberties of England."* Now what? Battle? Death? Or defeat and capture? She must have shuddered as she remembered that other rising in the West Country only three years before, when the Duke of Monmouth's hopes had melted into the fog and cannon smoke of Sedgemoor. They had cut off his head. . . . What would happen to William if he, too, failed?

William did not fail. He was a better soldier, and those three years of James's government had swung whole sections of the community—and whole regiments of the army—against the King. But England did not fall as easily as Jericho. There were weeks of uncertainty when even William wondered, and stole a glance over his shoulder toward the friendly sea. Those weeks must have been far worse for his wife, alone in that palace amid the silent, wintry oak woods.

William was not a particularly good correspondent when he was away, but it was not just that he was too busy, still less that he was neglectful. It was primarily to save her from worse worry on his behalf. When he was about to fight a battle or begin a siege, he used to keep the news from her. So now, when supporters came trickling only slowly into his camp at first, when there were ominous reports of the troop movements against him, and when he realized that the whole operation was to be a touch-and-go affair, he did not pour out his private thoughts in letters home.

It turned out all right in the end. Mary heard how

the resistance had crumbled, how her father had fled, how William was in London with his troops. But then there were more weeks of waiting before she could be reunited with him. There was so much to be settled. . . .

Parliament was making difficulties. Who was to be sovereign in place of the fugitive James? Many people wanted Mary to be proclaimed Queen by herself. William refused to take second place to his own wife, and Mary warmly supported him. She had no desire for the crown. She would sooner have left the throne vacant, with William acting as regent. But, if that would not do, she and William must be joint rulers.

Finally this latter arrangement was agreed upon, and in February, 1689, Mary set out to join William in England. Curiously enough, just as she had fallen deeply in love with the husband chosen for her, so she had come to love the foreign country which had once seemed to her a place of exile, and now she was most unhappy to leave it.

"It would be hard," she wrote in her journal, "for me to express the different emotions I felt in my heart at the sight of my own native country. I looked behind and saw vast seas between me and Holland that had been my country for more than 11 years. I saw with regret that I had left it and I believed it was forever; that was a hard thought, and I had need of much more constancy than I can brag of, to bear it with patience." When she met William, "as soon as we were alone we both shed tears of joy to meet, and of sorrow for meeting in

England, both wishing it might have been in Holland, both bewailing the loss of the liberty we had left behind and were sensible we should never enjoy here; and in that moment we found a beginning of the constraint we were to endure here after, for we durst not let ourselves go on with those reflections, but dried up our eyes lest it should be perceived when we went out."

So, at twenty-seven, Mary II was crowned the rather reluctant Queen of England. She had left her country as a pretty girl of fifteen: she came back as a handsome, stately woman, still slender, still young. Indeed, she was never to be really old, though the heavy fashions and elaborate hair styles of her time, combined with her taste for gloomy religious reading and complicated embroidery, make us think of her as older than she ever lived to be. In a sense perhaps Elizabeth was younger at sixty than Mary at thirty.

Her life as Queen was not easy. She could not avoid state business now. "My opinion having ever been," she wrote in her journal, "that women should not meddle in government, I have never given myself to be inquisitive into those kind of matters."* But, like it or not, she had to take charge when William was away—and he was away a great deal. James had to be fought and beaten in Ireland, where his chief support lay, and where the serious fighting in the Glorious Revolution took place. So, while William was away winning the Battle of the Boyne, and

* Mary's grammar was sometimes uncertain.

later, on the Continent, losing the Battle of Steinkirk against the French, Mary had to do her best. Usually William approved her decisions afterward. It seems generally agreed that Mary made a much better queen than anyone could reasonably have expected, in view of her ignorance and her gentle character.

"Let the Queen rule you," William once burst out in a fury to his English councilors. "She is English. She understands what you want. I don't."

Some of them would have been only too glad to take him at his word. Mary was popular with her people—but, for that matter, she had been wonderfully popular with the Dutch. Her goodness and virtue appealed to the mass of her British subjects, who had been disgusted by the scandals of the court during the past thirty years. If Mary had lived as long as Victoria, she might have been almost as successful in cleansing public life, though she would never have had Victoria's firmness in imposing her own standards on the court. As it was, her quiet example—even for those few years—was like a breath of purer air.

She was probably the first prominent member of the British royal family to take that active interest in hospitals, charities, and good causes which has been such a marked characteristic down to the present day. Religious societies were just coming into existence at the turn of the century, and Mary did much to help them.

For the rest, as a home-loving woman, she found her chief happiness in quiet ways. It was she who started the fashion in England for collecting porcelain, and made chintz and printed calicoes popular as materials. Following her example, people began to use more and more walnut in furniture, instead of the traditional oak—the typical "William and Mary" period piece is made of that wood. A good deal of such furniture was actually imported from Holland, and many suites were designed in England by Daniel Marot, the great Huguenot craftsman who came over to work for Mary. She started a vogue, too, for lacquered furniture, copied from the actual Chinese examples imported by the Dutch East India Company. William himself is said to have brought grandfather clocks into England.

Gardening was one interest which the King and Queen could share. They brought new ideas and new plants into the old English garden. Some of their followers probably went too far in trying to copy the formal, geometrical Dutch garden. They provoked the *Spectator* to complain, a few years later: "Our trees rise in Cones, Globes and Pyramids. We see the Marks of the Scissors upon every Plant and Bush. . . . I would rather look upon a Tree in all its Luxuriancy and Diffusion of Boughs and Branches than when it is thus cut and trimmed into a Mathematical Figure." William and Mary, however, had schemes beyond clipped yew hedges and straight paths of colored gravel. They brought over orange trees and citrons from Holland to fill their new orangery at Hampton Court, they received flower roots from New England, and sent their gardeners as far as the Canary Islands and Virginia to fetch back new varieties.

William's poor health made London unsuitable for him to live in. More and more houses were burning coal, which was brought by sea from the northeastern collieries, and the sooty, foggy atmosphere was bad for his asthma. Mary, too, disliked the dark old palaces of Whitehall and St. James's, with their uncomfortable memories; not only had she now no contact with her father and stepmother, exiled abroad, but her relations with Anne were chilly, and the two sisters never met, owing to Anne's friendship with Sarah Jennings (by then become Lady Marlborough) of which Mary strongly disapproved.

Altogether, both William and Mary were only too glad to make a fresh start. They had one home at Kensington Palace, now long since swallowed up in London but then in the country, and another at Hampton Court, some miles upriver, where they carried out a great many improvements. In both palaces it is still possible to see the rooms they occupied, and a lady of that time, Celia Fiennes, has left us a vivid description of the second. She writes:

"I went to Hampton Court 10 mile from London. It looks like a little town, the buildings run so great a length on the ground, the old buildings and the new part which King William and Queen Mary built. The Queen took great delight in it. . . . There was the Water Gallery that opened into a balcony to the water and was decked with china and fine pictures of the Court ladies drawn by Kneller. Beyond this came several rooms and one was pretty large; at the four corners were little rooms like closets or drawing-rooms, one panelled all with japan, another with looking-glass, and two with fine work under panels of glass." Later she describes the Queen's closet, with its "hangings, chairs, stools and screen the same, all of satin stitch done in worsteds, beasts, birds, images, and fruits all wrought very finely by Queen Mary and her Maids of Honour." Celia Fiennes takes us through the palace room by room, into "the Presence chamber, with a low screen across the room to keep company off the bed, which is scarlet velvet with gold orris" (a kind of lace embroidery), down the long gallery with its marble tables and couches covered with green and white damask, into the State Room with William's full-length picture over the mantelpiece, and into the drawing room where Mary's own portrait was hung.

It was a sad, unfinished home that Celia Fiennes visited. For Mary, whose delight it had been, had died a year or two before. William had not had the heart to go on with the rebuilding and refurnishing. The work stopped abruptly, and it was not resumed for five years.

Death came suddenly to Mary, at their other palace of Kensington, at Christmas, 1694. She fell ill a day or two before the festival, and on Christmas Day it was confirmed that she had smallpox, of a particularly severe kind. It was typical of Mary that she at once asked all those who had never had the disease to leave the court and escape the infection. On December 28 she died. She was not yet thirty-three.

Then it was that William's iron reserve broke down, and he amazed everyone by the passion of his grief. Then at last it was possible to guess how much more she had meant to him than anyone—even perhaps herself—had ever realized. Long afterward, when he was advised to marry again as most widowed kings had done before him, he whipped round upon his councilors.

"If you have forgotten your mistress," he said, "I have not."

ŏŏŏŏŏ

ANNE: THE EIGHTEENTH-CENTURY QUEEN

At daybreak on Sunday, March 8, 1702, an excited bishop burst in upon Anne and her ladies as they sat, drowsy and worn after a night of waiting, in a room at St. James's Palace. Bishop Burnet had driven at breakneck speed from Kensington, where King William had just breathed his last.

Anne was Princess no longer, but Queen of England—the last Stuart to reign and the first of the eighteenth-century sovereigns.

For, with Anne, we seem to pass into a new age. The changes which are at work in William and Mary's time have now gone far enough to produce a noticeable alteration in English life. We are now fully launched into the century of sedan chairs and snuffboxes, fans and face patches and full-bottomed wigs, coffee houses and Fleet Street journalism, red-coated soldiers and pipe-clayed belts, and a dozen other things which we associate especially with the eighteenth century

Addison and Steele are about to launch the *Tatler* and the *Spectator*. Swift and Defoe are writing, though *Gulliver's Travels,* and *Robinson Crusoe* will not be published until the next reign. Alexander Pope is about to establish—with his elegant and highly polished couplets—the pattern of the new poetry.

Purcell is dead and most of the other composers who sprang up in the great revival of music after the Restoration; but very soon London is to be electrified by the operas of a remarkable young man from Germany named Handel, who is to set the standard of English musical taste for the next hundred years.

Meanwhile, in the homes of the people, the tendency toward simplicity, light, and cleanliness (the Dutch ideals) makes further headway. The "Queen Anne house" remains, to this day, the ideal of many discriminating English people. Furniture begins to lose its old heaviness and to achieve a new elegance of line, paving the way to the great designers, Chippendale, Hepplewhite, and Sheraton, later in the century.

Despite all the great mansions which are still to be built, and all the vast parks to be laid out round them—despite all the homage paid to the nobility—this is more and more the age of the rising middle class. After all, the most magnificent of all the new mansions is Blenheim Palace, built for the newest of the dukes, Marlborough, a former nobody named John Churchill.

"Here," cries the great writer Voltaire a few

years later, coming to England from the still feudal France, "talents are the passport to glory!"

Rank and gentility are of tremendous importance, but a humbly born man can win his way on merit. Only a few may become lords or bishops, but there are thousands of others well satisfied with minor successes. Between them they are creating a new England—a more enclosed and better farmed countryside, brighter and more elegant towns, and a commercial greatness which spreads farther and farther, year by year, around the globe.

There are now five and a half million people in the kingdom. Half a million of them live in London—a London already dominated by the half-finished mass of St. Paul's Cathedral and prickly with the graceful spires of more than fifty other churches* built, since the Great Fire, by Sir Christopher Wren.

Such is the England of which Anne, on this wintry Sunday morning, has suddenly become Queen.

And what was she like herself, this younger sister of Mary, the onetime cherubic little girl who played Nymphe in the masque of Calisto?

Born on February 6, 1665, in that terrible year of the Plague, Anne was now thirty-seven. She still looked more of a Hyde than a Stuart. Her face was still round, but time had given it a more serious expression. She had light gray eyes and

* Churches of this period are rare elsewhere in Britain, but more common in New England, for Queen Anne took an interest in the religious life of her American colonies. She received four Mohawk chiefs at her court, and arranged for missionaries to be sent out to the Red Indians.

dark brown hair, piled up high in the elaborate fashion of the day. She was moderately tall, and had not yet become really fat. This came later, and was partly a tendency inherited from her mother, partly the result of bad health and too little exercise.

On that day of her accession she was already in mourning, but she had always a plain taste in clothes and, unlike Mary, disliked jewels. She was fond of music and played the guitar well. When not thus employed, her hands (and they were outstandingly beautiful hands, we are told) were perhaps happiest when shuffling and dealing the cards. Unfortunately, she suffered a great deal from gout as time went on, both in her fingers and in her legs.

This gout also interfered with her outdoor pleasures. Unlike her sister, but like Queen Elizabeth on whom she tried to model herself, Anne loved hunting—which still meant the stag, for fox hunting had scarcely begun. But where Elizabeth had ridden hard to hounds all her life, the still youngish Anne had to content herself with driving through Windsor Forest in a carriage.

Horse racing also delighted her. All the Stuart kings had patronized the sport, and her uncle Charles II, in particular, had made Newmarket fashionable, after the Puritan ban on race meetings had been removed. Few ladies, however, were to be seen at the races. Anne not only went to Newmarket but, after she became Queen, established the famous meeting at "royal" Ascot, nearer London, which remains one of the high lights of the social season. She ran horses in her own name and gave gold cups and plates as prizes. If it was Mary who started the tradition which links the ladies of the royal family with charitable societies, it was Anne who brought them actively into horse racing.*

Thus, it was not only in face but in character and interests that the two Stuart sisters were different. It is easy enough to understand this when we remember that they were together only in childhood, and not always, even then.

Their early years at Richmond Palace and St. James's followed roughly the same pattern, except that between the ages of three and five Anne was in France, staying first with the Queen Mother and then with her Aunt Henriette, who was married to the brother of Louis XIV. She was sent there for her health (particularly for her eyes which, however, remained very weak all her life), but the English people were so violently anti-French that the news of her long visit had to be disguised and the public were told that she was away at the seaside. They need not have worried. Anne was never to waver in her Church of England beliefs, and her armies, when she grew up, were to shatter those of France. Not even King Louis' parting present of two diamond bracelets left any lasting effect on the little girl's mind. As we have seen, jewels meant little to her.

* Her present Majesty has taken over the late King's horses and colors, but before that, as a Princess, she shared the ownership of a race horse with her mother.

Home in England, Anne soon acquired an older girl friend, to whom she was as passionately devoted as Mary had been to Frances Apsley. But whereas, in Mary's case, the friendship faded naturally away as the girls grew up, separated, and married, in Anne's it lasted a great part of her life and had a most unfortunate effect upon it.

The friend was the vivacious, strong-willed, ambitious Sarah Jennings, who later married John Churchill and became Duchess of Marlborough, an ancestress of Winston Churchill.

When they first met, Sarah was twelve and Anne eight. It was natural enough that the younger girl should fall under the spell of the elder.

The friendship was strengthened at the time Anne lost the company of her sister, when Mary married and went to Holland. The two Princesses must have been deeply attached, whatever their other friendships, for when Mary sailed with William the news had to be kept from Anne (then ill with smallpox) and supposed messages and inquiries from Mary were sent to her every day, until she was sufficiently recovered to bear the truth.

The childhood days at Richmond were over now, and she lived more with her father and beautiful stepmother, who were still Duke and Duchess of York. Once, driving back to Windsor with the Duchess, she had an alarming little adventure. They had been to visit the Duke of Buckingham at Clifden and, as they had stayed unusually late, the coachman and other servants had been rather too well entertained belowstairs. So, when they started on the return journey, they were in no state to drive their mistress safely over bad roads in the darkness. The coach rumbled on, zigzagging without much reference to the ruts and potholes in front, and the young ladies were flung heavily against each other. Then, suddenly, it heeled over at a really terrifying angle, and overturned with a crash. The servants, sobered and horrified, scrambled to their feet and ran shakily forward, some to quiet the horses, others to help the ladies out of the coach. To their unspeakable relief nobody was seriously injured. The Duchess had hurt her nose and Anne's face was bruised. That was all.

A few months later they paid a private visit to Mary in Holland, and Anne had her first real experience of foreign travel, since she had scarcely been old enough to remember much of France. In the following year, when she was fourteen, she made another visit to the Continent.

In this case there was an important reason. England had been lately stirred by fresh rumors of Catholic conspiracy. A man named Titus Oates had produced a highly dubious story of a plot to murder King Charles, burn London, massacre the Protestants, and bring in French troops to establish the Roman Church. The fantastic story had grown until even the Duke of York came under suspicion, and the King, though not believing a word of it, had to ask Anne's father to go abroad for his own safety. Anne was not allowed to go with him, but later she was given permission to visit him in Brussels, then part of the Spanish Netherlands.

Besides seeing her father and stepmother, Anne was delighted to be with Sarah once more. This young lady was now married to Colonel Churchill, who was serving as one of the Duke's Gentlemen of the Bedchamber.

Anne's impressions of foreign travel are preserved in some letters to Lady Apsley and her daughter Frances. They are not so very different in style from what a modern girl of her age might write. "It is a great and fine town methinks; though the streets are not so clean as they are in Holland, yet they are not so dirty as ours. They are very well paved and easy, they only have odd kinds of smells. . . . The Park here is very pretty, but not so fine as ours at St. James's. . . . I saw a ball at court which far surpassed my expectations, for it was very well. There we had lemonade, cinnamon water, and chocolate sweetmeats, all very good." On another evening she greatly enjoyed the bonfires and fireworks which celebrated the wedding of the King of Spain. But in time she tired of sight-seeing. "This place affords no news. . . . All that one has to do here is going to fine places to walk."

It was the same cry later when her father moved to Scotland and she made the five-day voyage up the North Sea coast to stay with him at Holyrood House in Edinburgh. "Write me all the news you know," she begged one of her friends. "Send me the *Gazette,* and other printed papers that are good." Her father was playing golf, still an essentially Scottish game. Her stepmother went riding with her most days until the older woman had an accident and hurt her leg. Anne herself continued riding and country-dancing, watching plays acted by Irish touring companies, and taking part in amateur theatricals herself. In May, after ten months in Scotland, she went back to London with her parents.

She was now seventeen. The second "glorious nymph" was ripe to be disposed of in marriage.

She had, in fact, been inspected eighteen months before by Prince George of Hanover, a cousin, descended like herself from James I and destined (had they but known) to follow her on the throne of England as King George I. But the German side of the family were snobs and despised Anne because her mother had been a commoner, so the Prince went home to Germany and married a more aristocratic cousin, Sophia Dorothea of Celle, in Prussia.

Anne never liked her Hanoverian relatives and, when she became Queen, blocked any proposal that they should come to England.

If she was not considered good enough for Prince George she was certainly too good for a more romantic suitor who next appeared. This was John Sheffield, Earl of Mulgrave, who at thirty had won a considerable reputation (though not entirely a good one) for his success with the ladies. As Groom of the Bedchamber to King Charles, he was continually meeting Anne at court and had ample opportunity to pay her attentions, sending her letters and songs of his own writing. The gossip reached even Mary at the Hague. Then the King put his foot down. The dashing Earl was dismissed from court and posted to the English base at Tangier.

One biographer even points out that he was sent there "in a leaky vessel," but perhaps there is no sinister significance in that. He appears at least to have arrived safely, but he troubled Anne no more. He was, however, one of the first to congratulate her on the morning of her accession, and she must have liked him a great deal, for she made him Duke of Buckingham and appointed him one of her ministers.

Had she some of that same wistful feeling for him that Elizabeth had always retained for the Earl of Leicester? She would have been no woman if the thought had never crossed her mind of how different life would have been with Mulgrave instead of the husband who was allotted to her.

There were only two serious objections to Prince George of Denmark. He drank too much and was very stupid. "I've tried him drunk and I've tried him sober," said Charles II sardonically, "but, 'od's fish, there's nothing in him."

There were two points in his favor. He was a good-looking, fair-haired Dane and he was a brave soldier. When his brother Christian, the King of Denmark, had been captured by the Swedes at the Battle of Lunden, it was George who had cut his way through and rescued him.

Unfortunately, as time passed (he was now thirty and Anne eighteen), these advantages had less chance to show themselves, whereas his drawbacks became more and more obvious.

They were married on July 28, 1683. Once more it was a late evening wedding—at ten o'clock—at

St. James's Palace, but it was a happier occasion, for Anne seems to have genuinely liked her big, simple Scandinavian. Royal weddings were arranged very differently in those days: the young couple went off to the theater together beforehand, with the Duchess of York, and returned just in comfortable time for the ceremony. The Bishop of London performed it, and the King, not her father, gave the bride away —which was appropriate enough, for the match was Charles's, and James could feel no enthusiasm at his second daughter's marrying a Protestant. But there was enthusiasm enough outside in the streets, as innumerable bonfires flared up to the summer sky, and, all over London, Wren's new-built steeples rocked with the pealing of the bells.

One would-be poet demanded:

What means this royal beauteous pair,
This troop of youths and virgins heavenly fair?
That does at once astonish and delight
Great Charles and his illustrious brother
here. . . ."

Great Charles was no more astonished than his illustrious brother was delighted. After all, he had arranged it. And, on the whole, the marriage turned out to be reasonably happy, though no "troop of youths and virgins" ever appeared to bless the couple with a family.

There was no question of whisking Anne off to Denmark, far from home and friends. She and the Prince were to have their own household in

England, and one of the first things she did was to appoint Sarah one of her Ladies of the Bedchamber.

"Let me beg of you," she wrote, "not to call me 'Your Highness' at every word, but to be as free with me as one friend ought to be with another; and you can never give me any greater proof of your friendship than in telling me your mind freely in all things. . . ."

To put Sarah even further at her ease, Anne hit on the idea of their calling each other, in private, by invented names. She herself became "Mrs. Morley." Sarah was "Mrs. Freeman"—was that name chosen as an allusion to Sarah's outspoken manner, or was the choice unconscious? Sarah needed no encouragement from Anne to speak her mind. She was a highhanded, tempestuous creature, who at sixteen had quarreled with her own mother and had her dismissed from court, and in later life was to cause trouble to a great many people, including Vanbrugh (who built the immense Blenheim Palace under her stormy eye) and Anne herself.

The newly married couple set up house at the Cockpit, which was part of Whitehall Palace, adjoining the orchard of St. James's Palace and flanked on one side by the old tiltyard and on the other by the tennis court where Henry VIII had once played with such vigor. But the first months were spent in traveling round the country. August saw them hunting the deer at Windsor. In September, at Winchester, they had their first experience of beagling, or hunting the hare, and went yachting from Portsmouth. Horse racing took them to Newmarket in October, and they returned to London for one of the severest winters on record. The Thames was so thickly frozen that coaches could ply along it between Westminster and the City. Stalls and booths were set up on the ice, turning it into a kind of fairground. Anne and her husband wandered through the muffled, rollicking crowds behind the laughing King.

Charles's rough gaiety was soon to be quenched. Almost exactly one year later, on Anne's twentieth birthday, he died suddenly and her father was proclaimed King James II.

The next few years were full of cares for the young Princess—cares both private and public.

She had already lost her first baby, a girl, born dead, but she had two more daughters, Mary and Anne Sophia, in 1685 and 1686. She wrote affectionately to her sister in Holland: "I have always forgot to thank you for the plaything you sent my girl, 'tis the prettiest thing I ever saw and too good for her yet, so I keep it locked up and only let her look on it when she comes to see me. . . . I will make it my endeavor always to make her a very dutiful niece." Within scarcely more than a month, however, both little girls were dead, Mary from some sort of wasting disease and Anne Sophia from no very certain cause.

The curse of ill-health, probably inherited from James II and due to his wild way of living, lay heavy on both his own daughters and prevented them from having healthy children of their own. It is sometimes said that Anne had seventeen children (even some good history books and encyclopedias make the statement), but in fact she had only six. The first was born dead, four died in infancy, and only one, William, Duke of Gloucester, born in 1689 just after the Glorious Revolution, reached the age of eleven, when he died suddenly of a "malignant fever." Even he had never been normally healthy.

So, as the Tudor line had ended with two childless sisters, Mary and Elizabeth, the Stuart was destined to finish likewise. The circumstances were different, but history repeated itself in the result.

Along with these family sorrows, Anne could not escape the general public anxiety during her father's short and stormy reign. She loved him and he preferred her to Mary, but, as a devout member of the Church of England herself, she was alarmed by his policy and afraid that he might try to begin the conversion of the heretic English with herself.

"The King has never said a word to me about religion since the time I told you of," she wrote to Mary, "but I expect it every minute, and am resolved to undergo anything rather than change my religion. Nay, if it should come to such extremities, I will choose to live on alms rather than change."

It is the voice, almost, of the other, the Catholic Mary. Again history repeats itself, but with a variation.

Anne had begun to dislike and distrust her stepmother, once her companion in so many rides and expeditions. "She is the worst hated in the world of all sorts of people," she told Mary, "for everybody believes that she presses the King to be more violent than he would be himself; which is not unlikely; for she is a very great bigot in her way. . . . She pretends to have a great deal of kindness to me, but I doubt it is very real. . . ."

Mary of Modena had been as unlucky with her children as Anne herself. When, therefore, in 1688 both the King and Queen appeared strangely confident that they would yet have a son who would survive to inherit the crown, Anne was among the numerous people who felt highly suspicious. Suppose her stepmother arranged for some newborn baby boy—humble in birth but healthy—to be smuggled into the palace and passed off as her own? Anne believed that the Queen would stick at nothing. She began to spy on her, in an attempt to find out if such a plot were really being hatched. On one occasion, it is said, her stepmother was so irritated by her hanging about in the bedroom that she seized a hairbrush off the dressing table and threw it at her. Anne was merely strengthened in her suspicions.

On June 12—when Anne was conveniently away at Bath—it was announced that the Queen had given birth to a son. This was James Edward, later known as the Old Pretender. No one now will ever know for certain whether he was a trueborn Stuart or not. Most historians think he probably was. But Anne, like Mary, William, and most of the anti-Catholic party, persuaded herself that he was not. It was this supposed wickedness on her father's part which made her feel justified in deserting him when William came over.

William landed in Devon on November 5. Anne's husband went off with the King to Salisbury, where the army was concentrating to meet the invader. Anne had already written to William from London, wishing him success and telling him that her husband, Prince George, would soon be joining him. Meanwhile, the Dane showed no sign of disloyalty to James. As one messenger after another came into the royal camp with news of fresh officers, regiments, and noblemen deserting to the Prince of Orange, he showed amazement and shocked sympathy. *"Est-ce possible?"* he kept exclaiming. *"Est-ce possible?"* Then when the right moment came—Churchill had gone the day before, with five hundred troops—George, too, melted quietly away into the west.

"Is *'Est-ce possible?'* gone too?" said James contemptuously, as he read George's farewell note.

In London, Anne realized that the moment had come to make her own exit. The Queen paid her an angry evening visit at the Cockpit; it is said that she even struck her stepdaughter. When she had swept out, Anne went to bed as usual, telling the servants that she was not to be called until she rang. There was not a moment to lose. Sarah was to be arrested in the morning and soon her own turn might come. Luckily, an adventurous plan had already been made with the help of Dr. Compton, who, though then Bishop of London, had been a dashing cornet in the Dragoons in his younger days. This plan now went into operation.

Just after midnight, when all was quiet, Dr. Compton arrived outside with a hackney coach. Anne and Sarah, accompanied by one servant and the wife of another officer who had deserted along with Churchill, crept down the backstairs and out of the house. They walked to the coach, got in, and were driven off to the Bishop's house.

By eight o'clock the next morning, when Anne's other ladies were drawing back the curtains to reveal an empty bed and screaming hysterically that she had been murdered by the priests or kidnapped by the Queen, Anne was in fact jolting northward by coach. Ex-Cornet Compton, vastly enjoying this break from the routine of his bishopric, rode beside the coach with a drawn sword and with loaded pistols on his saddle.

As the journey continued, this armed escort grew to the size of a small army. Indeed, Anne's flight from her father brought in almost as much support in the Midlands as did William's advance against him through the South Country. By the time she reached Leicestershire there were hundreds of armed riders strung along the road. Everywhere it was like a triumphal progress. There was a welcoming banquet at Leicester, where the Bishop declared, apologizing for his warlike appearance: "I have been forced to lay aside the Bible at present, but hope very suddenly to take it in my hands again."

At Nottingham the militia turned out in force

and led the fugitive Princess into their town as though she were a conqueror. There was another banquet of welcome, given by the Earl of Devonshire and attended by all the local nobility. Anne was safe there and had no need to go farther. Soon came the news that her father, deserted on all sides, had given way to William and left the country. The revolution was over.

When the rejoicings had died down Anne found that the new order of things had its drawbacks.

It had been wonderful to see the triumph of her own religion, the departure of her scheming stepmother (as she now thought of her), and the return of her long-lost sister. But there were disappointments.

She had not seen Mary for years. As many other people have discovered since, it is all very well to keep up an affectionate correspondence from afar, but not so easy to avoid friction when one is in close personal contact.

Mary and Anne had been fond of each other as girls. Now they had grown apart in character and tastes. Mary, the more talkative, was yet the quieter in her interests; she did not share Anne's passion for hunting and other sports, while Anne, though a good churchwoman, had not Mary's fondness for heavy religious reading. Dancing and cards they did both enjoy, but Anne was a much more reckless gambler.

Nor did their husbands get on well. William despised George, and, though he agreed to make him the premier nobleman in England, he snubbed him on every possible occasion. Anne, in turn, disliked William and felt injured. After all, she argued, she herself came between Mary and William in the line of succession, and, by agreeing to their coronation as joint sovereigns, she had stood aside in William's favor. Surely she deserved some gratitude for that?

The Churchills—now the Earl and Countess of Marlborough—were an even greater cause for ill-feeling. So long as William was his own commander in chief there was little scope for the future victor of Blenheim to show his military genius. Even if William had been looking for a general to take over the allied English and Dutch forces, he would hardly, in those first years, have given the chance to John Churchill. He distrusted the man—not without cause. After all, he had fought for James II against the Duke of Monmouth in 1685 and deserted to William three years later. Might he not change sides again, if it suited him? There were some grounds for suspecting that he might.

This was the man whose wife lived with Anne and had such an influence over her. It was Sarah who had helped to organize that midnight escape *from* James II. Suppose there should come another night, another hackney coach—and the strong-willed Sarah should spirit her away, *back* to her forgiving father?

"Est-il possible?" as Prince George might have said. It was more than possible. The danger of a counterrevolution was very real. There were plans for James II to land in England at the head of a French army. At one time Marlborough was im-

prisoned in the Tower on suspicion of high treason, and Anne wrote to Sarah: "I am just told that as soon as the wind turns westerly there will be a guard set upon the Prince and me." But that crisis never came.

Mary was continually begging Anne to give up her dangerous friendship, and Anne always stubbornly refused. Neither would give way. Mary's devotion to her husband came before sisterly affection and so, with Anne, did her loyalty to Sarah. Mary finally sent a message through the Lord Chamberlain officially forbidding Sarah to live at the Cockpit, which, as an annex to Whitehall Palace, was really part of the court. Anne decided that in that case she too would go. She accordingly arranged with the Duchess of Somerset to have the use of her mansion, Syon House, about eight miles away.

Mary was furious at this and made it clear that anyone visiting her sister would incur her own displeasure. William withdrew the military escorts which had previously accompanied Anne and her husband when they drove out. This had a serious consequence, for one March evening, as Anne traveled home from London, her coach was stopped by highwaymen and she was robbed.

For the last year or two of Mary's life the sisters never met, though, when Mary was dying, Anne offered to go and see her. She was asked to postpone her visit, as it was important to keep the Queen as quiet as possible, and the end came so quickly that she never saw her again.

Strangely enough, Anne had better treatment from William reigning alone than she had received during Mary's lifetime. It may have been a genuine improvement in the feeling between them, or it may have been caution and common sense on his part. With Mary dead, Anne had (by birth) a better right to the English throne than he had. True, in 1689 Parliament had settled that the throne was not something to be passed on by divine right but rather something to be occupied, on terms, by agreement between sovereign and people. But England was still full of those old-fashioned enough to think of it in the old way. Anne was popular. If she was persecuted, there might be another rising—this time in *her* favor. Many who would not have sided with Anne against Mary would certainly have supported her against a Dutch outsider.

Whatever William's true motives, Anne was brought back into favor—up to a point. After a time she returned to live not at the Cockpit but at St. James's, where she led a gay social life, giving a ball each Monday and especially brilliant balls for such occasions as her son's tenth birthday. That was, apparently, one of the most lavish occasions for many years past. Anne's petticoat trimming alone had cost £500—and the noblemen were as splendid as their ladies, wearing scarlet with gold embroidery and other magnificent color schemes.

Early in 1702, riding in the grounds of Hampton Court, which Mary and he had loved so well, the King was thrown from his horse. His broken collarbone did not set properly, there were complications, and on March 8 he died. He, too, had been childless. Dr. Burnet, Bishop of Salisbury, leaped into a coach and hurried to St. James's, determined to be the first to kiss the new Queen's hand.

Not only was Anne Queen, but she meant to rule. She had no intention of being a simple womanly figure like her elder sister, merely serving as her husband's representative when he was absent. In any case, Prince George counted for nothing, politically.

Elizabeth Tudor was her model. She revived that monarch's motto, *Semper Eadem,* "Always the Same." Like Elizabeth, she was following a sister who had been married to a foreign ruler, and, just as Elizabeth had boasted that she was "mere English," Anne reminded her people that she was "entirely English," and won easy popularity with all who had been jealous of William's Dutch friends.

But there had been many changes in the century since the death of Elizabeth. The long battle between Crown and Parliament had been won by the latter. No longer could a sovereign struggle on, year after year, without calling Parliament. It now sat frequently, and the Glorious Revolution had shown it finally to be the supreme power in the country. True, modern democracy was still far away; the House of Lords meant more than it does now, and the House of Commons was elected by the votes of only the top layers of the population; and the party system was a rough-and-ready affair. But the fact remained: no king or queen of England would ever enjoy the same personal power that the Tudors and the earlier Stuarts had possessed.

Anne did not like to face that fact. She wanted to choose her own ministers and to follow her own policy. She could not prevent Parliament meeting frequently, debating, and voting, but it never occurred to her to do what a twentieth-century sovereign is compelled to do—keep an absolutely neutral position and consent to whatever is decided by the majority.

Anne saw the matter quite differently. Since this Parliament existed, she must make it go *her* way. And since it was made up, broadly, of two parties, the Whigs and the Tories, she must back whichever side represented her own views. She must fish boldly in the troubled waters of party politics.

She was the last English sovereign to attend the debates of the House of Lords. She was there, in theory, incognito—just listening, as a private person, in contrast to those occasions when she appeared in state to open a session. But there was no secret about it. Sometimes she actually sat on her throne; once, feeling chilly, she came down informally and sat on a bench by the fire. In this way she gained a detailed firsthand knowledge of public business and of the men conducting it.

What she did not learn that way she found out from her favorite political adviser, Robert Harley, who at various times was Speaker of the House of Commons, Secretary of State, and Chancellor of the Exchequer—the position of Prime Minister being as yet unknown. Even when Harley was not in the government, she used to receive him and consult with him secretly, behind the backs of her official advisers. England having no written constitution, there was no hard and fast rule to prevent her doing so.

In fairness to Anne we must remember this: if her conduct fell far below that of modern kings and queens, the politicians of her day fell equally far below the standards expected now. Politics can never be spotless and innocent in any age or country—but English politics in the eighteenth century were as dirty a game as they have ever been in the history of Parliament. Swift satirizes them savagely in *Gulliver's Travels.* Anne's interference would have been unforgivable today. At the time, it was probably more a good thing for the country than a bad one.

Needless to say, one of her first moves was to promote the Marlboroughs. On the Wednesday after William's death she drove to the House of Lords, with Sarah sharing her coach and John bearing the Sword of State in front of her. Within a few days he was honored with the Order of the Garter, appointed Captain-General of the allied forces (which included British, Dutch, and German contingents), and sent off to Holland with the powers of an ambassador, to hold the two countries together.

Sarah was heaped with other honors. She became Groom of the Stole, Mistress of the Robes, Keeper of the Privy Purse, and Ranger of Windsor Park—this last because she had always coveted the lodge which went with the office. Her two grown-up daughters became Ladies of the Bedchamber. It seemed as though the Churchill family, between them, were in full control.

John, at least, justified his promotion.

For most of Anne's reign England was engaged in the War of the Spanish Succession. She was fighting with her Dutch, German, and Austrian allies—"the Grand Alliance"—to stop France, for a long time the foremost land power in Europe, from absorbing the old Spanish empire and becoming the mistress of the world.

Sarah's husband was not only one of the greatest military geniuses England has ever produced: he was able to make opportunities for his talents to operate. He got on well with the other principal commander, Prince Eugene, so that, instead of wasting time in jealous wrangles, they were able to work together with perfect understanding. And he was able to handle the suspicious, cautious Dutch government, so that, although they wanted to keep their troops near home, he was able to get them halfway across Europe to the banks of the Danube. There at Blenheim, in 1704, with Eugene's help, he smashed a superior French army and captured its commander. It was the first time in sixty years that a French army had been really beaten.

The news came to Anne in the form of a note from John to Sarah, scribbled in pencil on the back of a bill: "I have not time to say more, but to beg you will give my duty to the Queen, and let her know her army has had a glorious victory. M. Tallard and two other generals are in my coach, and I am following the rest. . . ." Anne was delighted to think that he had justified her favor, in spite of his many envious critics. She had already raised him from an earldom to a dukedom, the highest rank in the nobility and one seldom given to anyone not of royal birth. She could raise him no higher, so, when Parliament asked that he should be suitably rewarded for his services, she gave him the royal lands at Woodstock, near Oxford, and set the architect Vanbrugh to build Blenheim Palace there to commemorate his victory.

The war, however, raged on. There were three other fronts on land—Spain, Italy, and the Netherlands—as well as the sea. Gibraltar was captured in the same month as Blenheim. Marlborough won further victories at Ramillies and Oudenarde; at Malplaquet he claimed a more doubtful one. France was pushed out of Italy and the Netherlands, but held on to Spain, and the allies held the sea. France got the worst of the war, but could not be knocked out finally.

Anne hated the slaughter. "Lord, when will this spilling of blood be at an end?" she was heard to exclaim. And when a French agent was secretly brought to see her with proposals, she said to him: " 'Tis a good work. I am sure I long for peace. I hate this dreadful work of blood."

It was not until 1713, near the end of her reign, that the Treaty of Utrecht was signed, putting an end to the war. France was so weakened that she never recovered until after the French Revolution. The Dutch were equally exhausted and their naval supremacy passed finally to England. England herself had collected Gibraltar, Newfoundland, Nova Scotia, and Hudson's Bay, as well as a monopoly of the slave trade with the Spanish American colonies and a right to sell other goods there.

Besides this, an Act of Union in 1707 had finally merged the two kingdoms of England and Scotland, previously linked only (and rather weakly) by the fact that they shared the same Stuart king or queen. Britain was now in truth a "United Kingdom," and well on the road to becoming also the center of a British Empire.

Anne had made her home at Kensington Palace, which suited Prince George's health, for he too, like William, suffered from asthma. The Queen drove daily to St. James's, much as a modern woman travels to work. Whitehall Palace had been burned down toward the end of William's reign; later its site was used for the various government offices we see today.

After work began on the great house at Blenheim, Anne saw less of Sarah, who was continually visiting the spot to harass the unfortunate architect. Anne needed friendship, and she turned more and more to her bedchamber woman, Abigail Hill. Abigail was a poor relation of Sarah, who had got her the place in the Queen's household. But she was also a cousin of Harley, Anne's favorite politician, and soon she improved her position still further by marrying Samuel Masham, Groom of the Bedchamber to Prince George.

Mrs. Masham had no great ambitions. She knew her place. And truth to tell, since she had got used to her power as queen, Anne had grown more and more irritated by Sarah's masterful ways. Sometimes she could not even lay hands on small sums of her own money. Sarah, as Keeper of the Privy Purse, would presume to lecture her on economy. Once, when she needed twenty guineas to pay for the funeral of an old servant who had died in poverty, she had to borrow the money from one of her ladies.

Sarah was furiously jealous when she found that her poor relative had taken her place as Anne's confidential friend. There were angry scenes, quarrels, accusations. The lifelong friendship cooled steadily until, after five or six years, Anne and Sarah were scarcely on speaking terms.

The Queen was afraid that the Duchess might publish those intimate personal letters she had written to her, long ago, in their "Morley" and "Freeman" days. She asked for them back. Sarah, realizing their value for blackmail purposes, refused to part with them.

The dispute became more and more an undignified petty wrangle, more worthy of small schoolgirls than great ladies. Sarah, made to give up her rooms in St. James's Palace, took away all the brass locks from the doors and the marble chimney pieces she had fitted there at her own expense. Anne retorted by stopping the building payments for Blenheim, declaring with some exaggeration: "I will not build a house for someone who has pulled down mine and gutted it."

She dismissed Sarah from her offices and demanded the gold key which was their symbol. The Duke of Marlborough went on his knees to her, begging forgiveness for his wife. But Anne was no longer under their spell. The Duke had to return to Sarah and report that an hour's pleading had been of no avail. Sarah unhooked the key and threw it across the room in a fury, telling him to take it.

In the end the Marlboroughs decided to go abroad. Sarah applied to Lord Dartmouth, the Secretary of State, for a passport. He sent her one with the Queen's own signature on it. Sarah sent it back contemptuously. If his own signature was not enough, she said, she would rather go without a passport at all. Neither she nor the Duke returned to England as long as Anne lived.

They had not long to wait in their self-chosen exile. It was December, 1712, and the Queen was nearing the end of her reign. Reports about her health were constantly circulating, and even rumors that she was dead. The phrase, "Queen Anne's dead!" has become a byword, still widely used as a scornful exclamation with which to greet stale news. When first coined, however, it had a rather different meaning.

Prince George had died some years before. Anne was childless and alone. Her father was dead, but her half brother, James Stuart, the Old Pretender, was across the Channel still claiming the English throne. The nearest Protestant heir was that other George, Elector of Hanover, who had thought himself too good to marry her in her youth. Anne had no love for this distant cousin, this German who knew no word of English, but no one else could carry on the Protestant succession.

Would the change take place without trouble? Would the English, who had not really liked Dutch William, accept this far more foreign king? Though not yet fifty, Anne was too tired and ill to worry herself, and she made no move to help George by allowing him to visit his future kingdom. It was for others to worry, those who would be alive to see. . . . And worry they did, wondering if each new false report of her death would be the signal for revolution and a landing by the Old Pretender.

On a July morning in 1714, Anne got up as usual about seven o'clock and had her hair dressed. Suddenly Mrs. Danvers, one of her bedchamber women, noticed that she was staring at the clock on the chimney piece with a strange, fixed expression. Frightened, she asked if the Queen saw anything unusual. Anne turned her head but could not speak. She collapsed, and almost at the same hour, just two days later, she died.

The brief golden age of Queen Anne was over, but a rich inheritance awaited her successors. The great century of Georgian England lay ahead, a vista ending in the small, far-off figure of Victoria.

THE YEARS BETWEEN

1714–1819

After Anne, came a long line of German Georges, Kings of Hanover who made little change in their outlook although they had become rulers also of Great Britain. George I and George II were followed by George III, whose policies provoked the American Revolution and whose lengthy reign ended with a period of madness and blindness. During these years England was ruled by his son, the Prince of Wales, as Regent (hence the term, Regency England), who later became George IV. This was an era rich in events. It was the age not only of George Washington but of James Wolfe, who conquered Canada for Britain; Robert Clive, who founded her Indian empire; and James Cook, who annexed Australia and New Zealand. Nelson at sea and Wellington in Europe led the victorious struggle against Napoleon. At home, the British fought for political liberties and the freedom of the press.

The two parties, the Whigs and the Tories, which had grown out of the looser Roundhead and Cavalier groupings, moved closer to the modern party system, in which they were to continue (changing their names in the nineteenth century) as the Liberals and Conservatives respectively. With the invention of power-driven machinery this period also saw the dawn of the Industrial Revolution. It was the age in which Handel wrote his Messiah *and Arne,* Rule Britannia; *Boswell his* Life of Johnson; *Sheridan,* The School for Scandal; *and Wordsworth, Coleridge, Blake, Byron, Keats, and Shelley, the bulk of their poems.*

♀♀♀♀♀♀

VICTORIA:

THE QUEEN-EMPRESS

"They are the worst millstones about the necks of any government that can be imagined," declared the Duke of Wellington—though, being the Duke of Wellington and famous for his barrack-room language he used a stronger adjective than "worst."

He went on, with a seasoning of oaths better left out here: "They have insulted—*personally* insulted—two thirds of the gentlemen of England. How can it be wondered at if they take their revenge on 'em in the House of Commons? It's their only opportunity, and I think they're quite right to use it."

The millstones were the royal family. The occasion was in 1818, when, to the delight of the Iron Duke, Parliament had thrown out a proposal to pay increased allowances to some of the King's younger sons when they got married.

That was how the majority of Englishmen felt about the royal family at the time. It was the atmosphere into which a princess, Alexandrina Victoria, was born just a year later, on May 24, 1819, in that same palace of Kensington in which Queen Anne had died, one hundred and five years before.

England had prospered in the meantime. Though she had lost her American colonies she had gained Canada, a large part of India, and other possessions. She had just won the greatest war in her history: Waterloo was a recent memory and Napoleon was still alive, exiled on a South Atlantic island. Yet never had the royal family been so disliked and despised.

What were the reasons?

The old King, George III, was pitied more than anything else. He was entering the last months of his sixty-year-long reign. He was blind, deaf, and insane. His past faults no longer stirred people to indignation—it was so long since the Declaration of Independence in 1776, so long since his stubborn stupidity had goaded the American colonists to revolution. But, if he was too old and feeble to be blamed, he was equally unable to inspire love or respect.

His kingly duties were carried out for him by the Prince Regent, soon to succeed him as George IV. "Prinny" had once been popular enough to win a nickname. He was, at least, a full-blooded, fast-living, gay dog of a prince, who had charmed one section of English society while shocking the rest. But of late years he had gone to pieces, grown absurdly and revoltingly fat, and disgusted even many of his old followers by the natural coarseness which lay beneath his thin cover of elegance.

"Prinny" was the eldest of the King's fifteen children. Eleven of the others were still alive. Whereas he, at least, served as Prince Regent, the others did little or nothing to earn their keep. They were, as the Duke remarked, millstones about the necks of the government.

They had not, up to then, even provided the King with any grandchildren to carry on the royal line. What would happen when George III died, as soon he must? The crown would pass first to the childless Prince Regent; then, at his death (and he was neither young nor healthy), to each of his surviving brothers and sisters in turn. There might be a fresh coronation every year or two, as one elderly, childless sovereign followed another. And then what—when the last died?

The whole situation was ridiculous.

It was not surprising if many intelligent Englishmen turned to the idea of a republic. If the royal line was to die out in any case, why wait? Why put up with these expensive, ill-mannered, and often immoral German princelings for another twenty or thirty years?

For German they were, through and through. George I had had only a little Stuart blood. Each of his successors—even George III, who "gloried in the name of Briton"—had taken a German wife. Though the Hanoverian kings had learned to talk English, they had become even more German in blood, rather than less.

Elizabeth had boasted that she was "mere English," Anne that she was "entirely English." Few people remember today that the third of the great queens, Victoria, was almost entirely German, and that her successor, Edward VII, a monarch of our own twentieth century, was, if possible, slightly more so.

That Victoria triumphed over these circumstances —that she made the royal family loved and respected, and made herself the living symbol of the British Empire—was the really personal achievement of her reign.

Her father was Edward, Duke of Kent, the King's fourth son. He was no more attractive than the other Hanoverian princes. Once, as commander in chief, he had sentenced a soldier to nine hundred and ninety-nine lashes. Again, at Quebec—for he had spent some time in Canada—he had sentenced another man to death for desertion and mutiny. He had made the prisoner dress in his grave clothes and march two miles to the gallows, with the coffin carried before him and the band playing a funeral march behind him. At the end of this ghastly ceremony the Duke graciously informed him that his life would, after all, be spared.

It is small wonder that such princes did not win the hearts of their subjects, and a great mercy that the future Queen grew up without the influence of such a father. For he died while she was a baby, so that she inherited only his blood, not his ideas of discipline.

A much greater influence was, naturally, her mother, Victoria Maria Louisa, Princess of Saxe-

Coburg-Saalfeld. She had been married before to the Prince of Leiningen, ruler of a petty German state, and had two children, a boy, Charles, who had succeeded his father at Leiningen, and a girl, Feodore, who was twelve when her half sister Victoria was born.

The Duke of Kent married this young widow without any marked enthusiasm. Two of the other royal millstones, his brothers, married about the same time and with the same idea. The House of Hanover must somehow continue. Within a year or two the dying King was at last a grandfather, several times over. One of the other babies came before Victoria in the line of succession, but lived only for three months. When the Duke of Kent died of pneumonia in January, 1820, and it was certain that Victoria would never have a brother to displace her, it became very probable that, if she lived long enough, she would be Queen of England.

The Duke died at the South Devon seaside resort of Sidmouth. From there, the Duchess and her baby daughter returned to Kensington Palace, where they had a suite of rooms which was their home for the next seventeen years. With them lived Feodore, fast developing into a lovely girl, with a natural tendency to spoil her plump little blue-eyed sister. And there was Feodore's governess, Fraulein Lehzen, daughter of a poor German pastor—described by Dr. Edith Sitwell in her Victoria of England as "a very soberly dressed parrot, with her sharp black eyes snapping . . . with her bird-thin mouth that was drawn in because of her habit of eating caraway seeds, with her glossy black head cocked on one side so that her sharp ears might catch any whisper, any rumor of indiscreet conduct. . . ." She became Victoria's governess too and a great influence over her, and "Prinny" (now George IV) tossed her a Hanoverian title with good-humored contempt, so that she became Baroness Lehzen, though there was no Baron Lehzen to match.

The mother was in striking contrast to the governess.

Here was no black-eyed parrot, but a brown-eyed, brown-haired, rosy-cheeked, bustling, fat little woman, fond of gay colors and fonder of talking than listening. The governess tried hard to be discreet, though she did not always succeed; the Duchess did not even try, and was continually causing upsets in the royal family.

Such were the influences—almost entirely feminine—which surrounded the Princess in her girlhood.

George III she had never known, for he had died within a few weeks of her father, long before her first birthday. But she had a vivid early memory of George IV, who invited them all to spend a few days at Cumberland Lodge, Windsor, when she was seven. He himself was living at Royal Lodge, and there they went to call on him.

He was a grotesque figure by then. He was immensely fat. Still clinging to eighteenth-century fashion, he wore a wig and she noticed, as she kissed his cheek, that it was thick with make-up. But he was kind and friendly.

"Give me your little paw," he told her. She called him "Uncle King," and he gave her an Order to pin on her left shoulder, a miniature of himself set in diamonds.

The next day, as the Kents were driving to Virginia Water, they met him going the same way with his sister-in-law, the Duchess of Gloucester, in his sporting, lightweight phaeton, with his servants magnificent in the blue and scarlet livery that was for the King's men alone.

"Pop her in!" he ordered jovially. Victoria ("Drina," they called her in the family, from her first name) was handed up and tucked in between her uncle and aunt. She waved excitedly to her anxious mother, and the phaeton dashed off at a spanking pace. It was all delightfully alarming, but the Duchess of Gloucester kept a protecting arm around her waist. They went bowling round one side of the lake and drew up with a flourish at a pavilion known as the Fishing Temple. Here they went aboard a barge and fished, while musicians played for them from another barge and crowds of people stared respectfully from the shore. Then there was tea with peaches at a lakeside cottage, and the wonderful day ended with a musical evening in the conservatory at Royal Lodge, turned into fairyland with colored lights.

"You shall choose the next tune," said Uncle King. "What's it to be, hey?"

She considered, and asked for *God Save the King.* Whether from tact or from lack of musical knowledge—or even from sheer exhaustion—it is now too late to inquire.

Altogether it was a most successful visit. The King liked his niece and was amused by her. Still more he liked the grown-up, lovely Feodore—but Feodore was now whisked off to Coburg by her German grandmother, to marry Prince Hohenlohe, and did not see Windsor again until another king was installed there. Even Fraulein Lehzen had his approval.

Though she was Victoria's governess she was not expected to teach her much in the way of ordinary book learning and what were called, in those days, "accomplishments." For these there was the usual team of tutors, captained by a clergyman, the Rev. George Davys, who had supervised her studies from the tender age of four. The organist of St. Margaret's, Westminster, came to teach her music and singing; a Royal Academician taught her to draw; a teacher from Westminster School struggled none too successfully to instill a knowledge of English grammar; there was a French dancing mistress for the minuet (ballroom dancing in couples, as we understand it, was only just coming in with the fashionable but rather shocking waltz, but it was not yet necessary for a princess to learn it, for she could not whirl round the room with any partner of common birth); there were other specialists for French and German, and, as she grew older, she was treated to lectures by scientific professors on such subjects as cohesion and capillary attraction.

Baroness Lehzen was more concerned with forming her character, which was good but by no means perfect. "Never have I seen such a passionate and naughty child," she declared more than once. But she was truthful, the Baroness admitted, at whatever the cost. Nothing would tempt her to lie. That was a deeply ingrained quality which time never altered. Not even kindness or courtesy would allow her to soften the literal truth. She always detested Gladstone, the great Liberal Prime Minister who served her and the country so honestly for more than half a century. Yet, when he came to say good-by for the last time—old and worn out in health—she could not bring herself to say "thank you" for what he had done. She was *not* sorry to see him go. Choosing her words carefully and alluding to his deafness and failing eyesight, she said: "I am sorry for the *cause* of your resignation." When he died, and the whole country paid tribute to him, she merely commented: "I never liked him, and I will say nothing about him."

When she said that, she was a Queen and a very old woman, nearing the end of her own course. But at the time of the Baroness's criticisms she was a small girl, strictly controlled, and not supposed even to suspect that she would ever wear the crown of England.

It was a common mistake of nineteenth-century parents and teachers to imagine that children knew only what was told them. Victoria was no fool. Any child of her age was quite capable of looking round the family, listing her uncles and aunts and cousins, and weighing her own prospects. If there was a fool at Kensington it was the Baroness, if she really believed that Victoria knew nothing of her future until she was eleven, when the Baroness coyly slipped a copy of the family tree inside her history book.

Victoria was only six when she told another small girl, Lady Jane Ellice: "You must not touch these toys, they're mine. And I may call you Jane, but you must not call me Victoria." And before she was nine Sir Walter Scott wrote in his journal, after dining at Kensington Palace: "This little lady is educated with so much care, and watched so closely, that no busy maid has a moment to whisper 'You are heir to England.' I suspect, if we could dissect the little heart, we should find that some pigeon or bird of the air had carried the matter."

George IV died soon after her eleventh birthday. Uncle William became King. Some called him "the sailor King," because he had served in the Navy under Nelson and was keenly interested in the sea. Others called him, less respectfully, "Silly Billy." He was not without common sense, though, and certainly not without kindly feelings. His chief lack was good manners.

Victoria did not go to the coronation—she spent the day in floods of tears, like any other disappointed girl. Her mother had started the seven-year wrangle with the new King which was to end only at his death and her daughter's accession. The Duchess of Kent was like a ruffled hen with one chick: all she could think of now was Victoria's rights and position as heir presumptive to the throne. She had begun by writing to the Duke of Wellington, as Prime Minister, demanding an allowance for her daughter from the King. The Duke had answered politely that the King fully intended giving her one, but he could do nothing till Parliament voted on the whole question of the royal incomes. There were further brushes between them, the Duke behaving as usual like a gentleman, the mother ignorantly, rudely, and absurdly, like any foolish woman determined to stand on her dignity and put her opponent in his place. On the matter of the coronation, King William was, strictly speaking, at fault. He arranged that, in the order of precedence, his brothers should come before her and her daughter; whereas, since her dead husband had been an elder brother, his widow and child should have occupied a similar senior position.

It is hard for those who have never lived in a stiff, formal society to appreciate how this question of precedence—the exact order of a procession, the seating at a banquet table, even the difference between driving in a carriage with one's back to the horses or facing them—can become a matter of life and death. It is still something which whitens the hair of diplomats and private secretaries. It was certainly not less vital in the England of 1830.

The Duchess stuck to her guns. She was not going to the coronation if it meant taking second place to her brothers-in-law. A child's passionate disappointment meant nothing. She took Victoria off to the Isle of Wight and wrote to say that the Princess was not well enough for either of them to attend.

William IV liked his niece and would gladly have

seen more of her. It was right that he should have done so, for he was an elderly man and it was practically certain that she would be the next sovereign. The Duchess was all in favor of preparing Victoria for what lay ahead—but any grooming of the future Queen was for her to do, with the help of her brother Leopold. He had just accepted the crown of Belgium, a newly created kingdom, but he liked nothing better than writing long letters of advice to his niece and was not unwilling to rule England, as well as Belgium, by remote control.

From the age of thirteen Victoria began to travel round the country with her mother, making herself known to the people who would one day be her subjects. They stayed at great country houses, such as the Duke of Devonshire's stately mansion at Chatsworth in the Derbyshire dales. King William lent his royal yacht to the niece he was scarcely allowed to see, and they sometimes traveled by water. Unfortunately, the Duchess insisted that artillery salutes should be fired every time she went aboard or came off the vessel, just as though she were the sovereign herself. The King did not wish to snub her publicly by forbidding these continual poppings and bangings, so it was hinted to her that she should give instructions, herself, that they were unnecessary. The Duchess refused. Once more, and this time quite literally, she stuck to her guns. It took an official Order in Council to silence them—and her. In future, the royal yacht was to be saluted only if the King or Queen was actually on board.

Victoria was now keeping a journal, so that her

life during her teens is very easy to picture. She wrote of her journeys and impressions; of her pony, "sweet little Rosa," and her mother's "dear sweet little Dash," a King Charles spaniel; of the new bridge she declared open at Chester and the cotton mills she visited in Derbyshire, and the foundation stone she laid at a boys' school in Wales. Nor did she leave out her assessment of the boy cousins who came over to visit her from Germany: "They are both *extremely tall.* Alexander is *very handsome* and Ernest has a *very kind expression.* . . . We shall miss them at *breakfast,* at *luncheon,* at *dinner, riding, driving, sailing, walking,* in fact *everywhere.*"

The habit of underlining almost every other word was one which remained with her in later years. She also resorted to a plentiful use of full capitals, and peppered her journals and letters with exclamation marks. She was always an emphatic person, and she knew no more subtle ways of making her opinion clear.

Birthdays, as might be expected, figured prominently in her records. "How *very old!!*" she wrote at fourteen. The King insisted on giving her a juvenile ball at St. James's Palace, and her mother could not very well refuse. It was a wonderful evening. The King led her in to supper himself, as the guest of honor, and the Queen sat on the other side of her, and everybody drank her health, and she danced no fewer than eight quadrilles, and it was well after midnight when she drove home to Kensington.

But how young fourteen seemed when she was sixteen! "I feel," she wrote, "that the two years to come till I attain my 18th birthday are the most important of any almost. I now only begin to appreciate my lessons, and hope from this time on to make great progress." This time the main birthday treat was a concert at Kensington Palace arranged by her mother, with all the stars from the Opera engaged.

Seventeen was marked by a ball, but a grown-up affair this time, and at Kensington, not St. James's. The Duchess of Kent was quite capable of giving a ball for her own daughter, without any help from the King. . . . This time the boy cousins who came over from Germany included Prince Albert of Saxe-Coburg, three months younger than herself, and she liked him best of all, which was fortunate because her scheming Uncle Leopold was already intent on getting them married. She finished the evening as his partner in a country-dance at half past three in the morning.

"Allow me then, my dearest Uncle," she wrote to King Leopold, "to tell you how delighted I am with him in every way. He possesses every quality that could be desired to make me perfectly happy. He has besides the most pleasing and delightful exterior you can possibly see."

The boy's impressions of the visit were given in a letter to his stepmother. The English climate made him bilious and he could not stand the long hours—he could hardly keep awake after midnight. "Aunt Kent was very kind," he added, "and our cousin also is very amiable." He was a serious, studious youth, and Victoria had not the intellect to meet him on his favorite ground—even her musical taste was superficial compared with his. But he had a strong sense of duty and would do what was expected of him.

There was one person who looked forward to Victoria's eighteenth birthday even more anxiously than she did herself. It was the King.

He was in failing health. The Duchess infuriated him more and more. "That woman is a nuisance!" he would cry, reading in his newspaper that she had been pushing herself forward again. His one fear was that he might die before his niece became eighteen and old enough to rule by herself. He could not bear to think of "that nuisance of a woman" acting, through her daughter, as the uncrowned Queen of England.

A climax arrived when they came to stay at Windsor the day before his own birthday banquet. Having public business in London, he paid a surprise visit to Kensington and found that the Duchess had moved into a suite of seventeen rooms, not only without his permission but in direct defiance of the orders he had given. Boiling with rage, he returned to Windsor and marched into the drawing room, where the family guests for the next day's banquet were gathered for the evening. He went first to Victoria, took both her hands affectionately, and declared that he only wished he saw her more often. Then he bowed coldly to her mother and remarked in a distinct voice, for all the room to hear, that he had just come from Kensington where "a most unwarrantable liberty" had been taken with one of his palaces. He did not understand conduct so disrespectful to him and he would not endure it. There was a painful silence after he had spoken. It was the stillness before the storm which broke at the birthday banquet next day.

It was a splendid occasion. There were a hundred royal and noble guests ranged along the tables. The myriad candles flickered softly on gold plate and jewels, on uniforms and sashes, on rich gowns and bare shoulders. Powdered flunkies stole about in the background or stood like statues. The King's health was drunk with due ceremony. Victoria faced her uncle across the table and smiled over her glass. Her mother, placed at his right hand, drank and was no doubt glad that he could not look into her eyes.

The King rose to make a speech in reply. And instead of the pleasantries usual on such an occasion, he let forth a stream of angry eloquence which paralyzed the diners and froze even the flunkies behind their chairs. If he had been an admiral, denouncing a mutineer from his quarter-deck, he could scarcely have said more.

The Princess Victoria would be eighteen next year. He hoped and prayed he might be spared for that period, so that there would be no risk of a regency by—he grew scarlet as his anger mounted—"a person now near me, who is surrounded by evil advisers and who is herself incompetent to act with propriety in the station in which she would be placed."

There was a gasp round the table. Queen Adelaide went pink with embarrassment. Truly, William had been sorely provoked, but really, a public banquet was no place—

The Duchess was white as death. Tears trembled in Victoria's eyes as her uncle went on.

"I have no hesitation in saying . . ." Certainly the rough-tongued old sailor had no hesitation: it was all too plain that he had very great pleasure. ". . . that I have been insulted, grossly and continuously insulted, by that person—but I am determined no longer to endure a course of behavior so disrespectful to me. Amongst many other things I have particularly to complain of is the manner in which this young lady has been kept away from my Court. She has been repeatedly kept from my Drawing-rooms,* at which she ought always to have been present—but I am fully resolved this shall not happen again. I would have her know that I am King and I am determined to make my authority respected. For the future I shall insist and command that the Princess do upon all occasions appear at my Court, as it is her duty to do."

The broadside had its effect. When the other guests had gone, the Duchess called for her carriage and declared she would drive back to London that night. She was persuaded, however, to stay at Windsor until the next day. She did not dare to ignore the King's words and from that time onward Victoria was regularly seen at court. But the King would see! Or rather—most unfortunately—he would not see, because he would be dead by then.

* Not the actual rooms, but the formal receptions held there.

Under or over the age of eighteen, Victoria was a dutiful daughter and, even when Queen, would always listen to her natural guide and adviser, that unselfish Mamma whose whole life had been given up to her protection and education, and whose bedroom she still shared wherever she went. What Mamma could not grasp herself would be taken care of by Mamma's dear brother Leopold. The child always listened to *him* with proper respect. "He is *so* clever, *so* mild and *so* prudent," wrote the Princess—was it entirely for her own satisfaction she wrote, or for her mother's eyes? "He alone can give me good advice on *everything*. To hear dear Uncle speak on any subject is like reading a highly instructive book. . . ." Is it possible that Victoria had more sense of humor than is sometimes supposed?

Her eighteenth birthday arrived. The King had been seriously ill, but he clung to life, if only to annoy his sister-in-law, and recovered sufficiently for the celebrations to take place as planned, though he was not able to attend the court ball given in her honor. He sent her a grand piano as a birthday present, and followed it with a direct offer—over her mother's head—of a ten-thousand-pound-a-year allowance. This vexed the Duchess. Four thousand pounds, she felt, would have been quite enough for so young a person, and the other six thousand should have been given to her, to spend on Victoria's behalf.

There was little time left for further squabbling. Within a few weeks it was known that the King's days were numbered, and on June 20, 1837, very early in the morning, he died.

"I was awoke at 6 o'clock by Mamma," wrote the new Queen in her journal, "who told me that the Archbishop of Canterbury and Lord Conyngham were here and wished to see me. I got out of bed and went into my sitting-room (only in my dressing-gown) and *alone,* and saw them."

That significant word *"alone"* is repeated over and over again in her entry for that first day of her reign. She saw Lord Melbourne, the Prime Minister —she held her first Council—she received four state officials—she had dinner . . . in every case, *alone.* She seemed suddenly a new person, with a power and dignity and independence which nobody (least of all her mother) had ever suspected. The Duke of Wellington, coming away from her Council, said: "She not only filled her chair, she filled the room."

There were many instructions to give on that first crowded eventful day, but there was one in particular which she must have waited—how long?—to give.

Her bed was to be moved out of Mamma's room. In future the Queen would sleep alone.

Mamma and "my *dear* Lehzen" and clever Uncle Leopold soon found that their influence was over. Leopold, writing long letters from Brussels, was naturally the slowest to realize it. His niece still answered charmingly, but it became clear that, having read his advice, she went her own way. She had accepted his agent, Baron Stockmar, as a confidential adviser, always at her elbow . . . but somehow Britain continued to go Britain's way, not Belgium's. This rather plain, stocky girl of eighteen —who lamented to her first Prime Minister, Lord Melbourne, "Everyone grows but me!"—was quite determined to rule.

Yet, though she had an iron will and a deep sense of her position as Queen, she had also (what Elizabeth I never had) a feminine longing to lean on a stronger, masculine arm. She had not, like the great Tudor, a passion for complete independence. She *wanted* to depend. But the person on whom she depended must be worthy, and chosen by herself, not by her mother.

In the first years of her reign she depended on Lord Melbourne—that charming, amusing, rather wicked old gentleman who taught her so much about public business, mixing his wise hints with jokes and compliments about her new tight sleeves or the fact that she had given up wearing her hair in curls.

But from the day of her marriage she depended more and more—at last almost entirely—on her husband. And after his death there was the third long phase of her reign when she depended not on any living adviser but on the memory of the dead, judging everything by what *he* would have done, what *he* would have wished.

The fourth phase was dominated by the Conservative leader, Disraeli, until he, too, died in 1881. Like Melbourne, he was witty and shrewd—but he far outdid Melbourne in the flattery of his compliments. Whenever Disraeli was in power, Victoria leaned happily on his support. When the Liberals won an election and her detested Gladstone took Disraeli's place as Prime Minister, she showed him only cold civility and longed for the next Conservative victory.

During that same period, in her private household, she depended to an extraordinary extent on a remarkable Highland servant, John Brown, whom she had promoted from a gillie, a sort of gamekeeper, to be her personal attendant. He was an outspoken, whisky-loving creature, who patted visiting statesmen on the back and addressed his royal mistress in more familiar terms than she would have borne from any other person alive; but she not only tolerated him, she liked him, and was grief-stricken when he died. The reason was partly that he had been her husband's gillie, his personal attendant on deerstalking expeditions at Balmoral, and that his death broke another link with Albert's memory. But there were many other people who had known Albert more closely, and they were not permitted the same liberties. Her treatment of John Brown was just another instance of this need to depend on someone—to have someone in the world who would give her instructions instead of receiving them, whether it was an adored husband, or a masterful servant bidding her drink up her tea.

Only in the last twenty years of her long reign was there no such dominating figure. But by then she was an old woman, fixed in her habits, ruling automatically, by instinct. Independent at last.

The story of Victoria is not the history of Victorian England.

The events of those sixty-three years cannot be fully told here, nor need they be, for they were not the Queen's doing. The time had gone by when an English queen could govern personally, almost without Parliament, as Elizabeth had done; or through a corrupt and managed Parliament, as—to a great extent—Anne and the Georges had contrived to do.

The First Reform Act, passed when Victoria was twelve, had wiped out any chance of that. Democracy was coming. The first years of her reign were stormy with the demands of the Chartists—votes for every man, however poor; secret voting; salaries for Members of Parliament, so that the working class could not only vote but provide their own candidates. Every one of the Chartist demands (except one, providing for a new Parliament each year) has since been granted and is now accepted as a natural part of the democratic heritage. But at that time these demands were revolutionary. Men armed and drilled to fight for them, men marched for them, and were shot down in the gutter. The Charter was refused at the cannon's mouth, but the demands in it were granted later, one by one.

By the end of her reign, democracy had arrived. Only the right of women to vote (of which she would have violently disapproved) was delayed a little longer.

Victoria favored some prime ministers much more than others. She did things which no modern queen would do. She was obstinate, she was sometimes interfering, but she never tried to fight Parliament or her ministers on any vital political question. She cannot be blamed—or praised—for most of the main happenings in her reign.

We are only concerned here with the part she was able to play in her own person.

First, coming to the throne as a gracious, well-bred girl, she made royalty popular as it had not been within living memory. Here, people felt, was no "millstone" but a sovereign they could love and respect.

Next, by her marriage and her family life afterward, she set a new and infinitely higher standard than any of her relatives. The accent was on goodness. England was tired of the drunken, gambling, loose-living Hanoverians. Hard work, plain living, and high thinking were the ideals of the period.

She married her cousin Albert early in 1840, before her twenty-first birthday. Remembering that she was a sovereign even before she was a young lady, she proposed to him. "Albert," she told the Duchess of Gloucester, "would never have presumed to take such a liberty as to propose to the Queen of England!" She was, not surprisingly, accepted.

"I will not let my courage fail," wrote the solemn youth to his tutor. "She is really most good and amiable, and I am quite sure Heaven has not given me into evil hands, and that we shall be happy together."

The wedding was small and quiet, not at the Abbey but at the little Chapel Royal of St. James's. She wore a white satin gown with a deep flounce of

Honiton lace, with earrings and a necklace of diamonds. There was a banquet at Buckingham Palace, a two-day honeymoon at Windsor with dancing both evenings after dinner, and then the conscientious Queen hurried back to her public duties in London.

The question was, what part in those duties—if any part—was her husband to play?

None, said the country firmly, or at most, purely ornamental. From the far-off days when Mary I had been married to Philip of Spain, the English had been determined that no foreign prince should edge his way on to the throne merely by marrying their queen. William of Orange was quite a different matter, for he had been one of the family anyhow.

Albert should never be King. Prince Consort was the highest title they would give him. He was an entirely worthy young man, without any vices—and the contrary English, being the English, never liked him.

Victoria, however, adored him. Not even Mary II had been more under the spell of her husband. Victoria could not hand over her power to Albert as Mary had done to William III—but not even the Prime Minister could prevent her talking every question over with her clever, thoughtful Albert, and afterward repeating his opinions as though they were her own.

So Albert became a mighty power in the background. He had to begin in a small way, overhauling the organization of the royal palaces with German thoroughness, suggesting how money could be saved by the dismissal of a footman here or the use of one candle instead of two. Launching out a little, he planned her a new house at Osborne, in the Isle of Wight, and then Balmoral, in the Highlands, a serious-looking mansion of granite, somewhat German in spirit but a wild riot of stags' heads and tartans inside. The chief architectural masterpiece he inspired, though, was the Crystal Palace, a really remarkable edifice of glass and bright blue iron girders, first erected for the Great Exhibition of 1851. The Exhibition itself was Albert's inspiration too: he had a boundless interest in science and industry, believing (like most men of his time) that humanity was moving steadily forward and that world peace and prosperity were just round the corner, to be achieved as soon as enough factories had been built and enough new inventions devised.

Gradually he began to have a greater and greater political influence. He worked tirelessly on the masses of papers which continually arrived for Victoria's signature. He explained, suggested, and phrased improvements. On the whole he was an influence for good. Without him, Victoria might have been more stubborn in her disagreements with her ministers.

Their first child was born in November, 1840. It was a girl, Princess Victoria, but a son and heir, Prince Albert Edward, followed a year later. Three more sons and four more daughters completed, in due course, a family of typical nineteenth-century size. Most of them grew up and married into the various royal houses of Germany or Russia, but only "Bertie"—later King Edward VII—played any important role in history.

"Bertie" was an interesting example of Victorian miseducation—Victorian being used here not in a personal sense but as the useful general adjective which it became, to express the whole outlook of that period, which Victoria and the Prince Consort did so much to form.

Fathers were to be looked up to, by mothers and children alike, as gods who knew everything and could do no wrong. The best thing that a boy could hope for was to be like his father.

No one believed in this more firmly than did Victoria.

It was also assumed that the right character could be built by using the right bricks and mortar—in the shape of rules, prohibitions, instruction, and supervision. The idea that human children are different and should be different, that they need freedom like plants to bend in the direction they prefer, never penetrated the royal nurseries.

Bertie was given the sort of upbringing his solemn father would have enjoyed. Unlimited opportunities for study, winding up with courses not at one university only but at three—Edinburgh, Oxford, and Cambridge—with a whole team of professors available to stuff him with lectures and book learning.

Bertie, however, did not much like books. He much preferred men and women. He had his own gifts, but neither of his parents could appreciate them. They bullied him and shook their heads over him, and he ended, like many of his generation, by revolting against them. His father had tried to make him a typical German, serious, conscientious, thorough; his father looked to a future in which Britain and Germany, as partners, would civilize the world. Bertie disliked the idea. He infinitely preferred the French. Long years afterward, as King, he was personally responsible for creating the Entente Cordiale—the Anglo-French friendship—which was to make the two nations allies in two wars against Germany.

Victoria's twenty-one years of married bliss were not matched by equal bliss for all her subjects. In 1845 the potato crop failed in Ireland and there was terrible famine. Three-quarters of a million people died, and, over the next fifteen years, two and a half million more emigrated to America, carrying with them a hatred of British government which smolders to this day.

From 1854 to 1856 there was the Crimean War, a pointless struggle between Russia on one hand and Britain, France, and Turkey on the other, of which little is now remembered but the equally pointless (though heroic) Charge of the Light Brigade, and the pioneer hospital work of Florence Nightingale. No sooner was peace made than the Indian Mutiny broke out, in 1857, with a sickening massacre of British women and children at Cawnpore and (what is less often taught in the schools of the West) counter-atrocities committed against the natives of India by the British.

The American Civil War opened in 1861, bringing unemployment to the Lancashire millworkers through the stoppage in the raw cotton supply. If it had not been for the Prince Consort, it might have had even more serious effects.

Two Southern envoys embarked for Europe in a British vessel. She was fired on and boarded by a Northern cruiser and the two Southerners were taken off as prisoners. Under international law this was wrong and there was great indignation in London. The fire-eating Lord Palmerston was then Prime Minister—another holder of that office whom Victoria had always detested, but had to accept. His Foreign Secretary wrote a dispatch in such strong language that, if it had reached Washington, it might have stung President Lincoln's government to declare war on Britain.

Albert saw the draft of the document before it went. He saw clearly what it meant. He was unwell at the time: he had caught cold inspecting the military college at Sandhurst, and he had just had a tiring journey to Cambridge to express his disapproval of Bertie's slackness. Ill though he felt, he settled down to the dispatch at seven o'clock in the morning, composing fresh phrases to soften the tone of it. Then he talked it over with Victoria, and she made one or two suggestions herself. The dispatch went back to Palmerston with their corrections, and "Old Pam," who had so often risked rapping the knuckles of foreign governments, had the sense to send off the revised, more diplomatic version. But by that time the Prince was really ill and had taken to his bed. The sickness proved to be typhoid, and two weeks later, on December 14, 1861, he died.

To Victoria it seemed that her own life was over. If anyone could have told her that nearly forty years of her reign still lay ahead, she would have found it unbelievable—and unbearable.

She had been wrapped up in her husband and not even her nine children could console her. She had always had a morbid interest in death—many young people had, in those days, when even a private person was buried with pomp and pageantry, and when mourning was a long-drawn-out drama of hushed voices and black clothes, with black edges even to handkerchiefs and writing paper. But few widows ever gave themselves up to grief as thoroughly as did Victoria.

For ten years she shut herself up in retirement. She could not bear to appear in public. She still carried out her unavoidable duties as Queen—signed papers, read memoranda, received her Prime Minister—but that was all. She was hardly ever in her capital. Busy statesmen, themselves often overworked or unwell, had to make frequent and exhausting journeys to see her in the Isle of Wight or the Highlands of Scotland. As middle-aged women sometimes do, the Queen persuaded herself that her nerves would not stand appearing at public functions or entertaining important visitors.

She would not do these things herself and she would not let her eldest son, Bertie, do them for her. The Prince of Wales was now married to the beautiful Alexandra of Denmark, and the young couple could very well have carried out all those social duties which the melancholy widow could not face. But they were not allowed to. Bertie was a failure, he had *not* turned out like his father, and he could not therefore be trusted with any responsibility. Victoria kept him so, idle and humiliated, until at last, when approaching his sixtieth birthday, he found himself a King.

In those years of retirement Victoria threw away most of the popularity—the love, even—which she had won from her subjects earlier in the reign. Again, but for new reasons, republican ideas became widespread. Why pay out huge sums each year, people argued, for a sovereign who holds no court and never drives out either to open a Parliament in state or to meet her people less formally?

It was, by a curious accident, her erring son who put a sudden stop to all that criticism. Bertie fell desperately ill with that same typhoid fever which had carried off his father. For two weeks he lay at death's door. The country waited breathless. All the former resentment against Victoria was swamped by sympathy. There were national rejoicings when he recovered, and a service of thanksgiving at St. Paul's, which the Prime Minister persuaded her to attend. Her drive to the cathedral was the cue for a tumultuous welcome from the crowd, and her old popularity came flooding back, helped by an incident two days later. She was leaving her carriage at the garden gate of Buckingham Palace when a fanatical Irish youth leveled a pistol at her. John Brown, the faithful Highlander, pounced on him. In a moment the youth was knocked off his feet and deprived of his weapon, which in any case proved to be unloaded. But it had *looked* like an attempt at assassination, it *might* have been fatal, and a new wave of loyalty swept through the country.

From then onward Victoria let herself be drawn back, step by step, into public life. When Gladstone was replaced as Prime Minister by the amusing and charming Disraeli, she was much more easily coaxed. She regained her old interest in affairs. She shared his dreams of a glorious, expanding British Empire.

It was expanding in earnest now. Since the Mutiny, India had come more and more under British control. The cutting of the Suez Canal through Egypt had strengthened the link, and Victoria was delighted when, in 1875, her clever Prime Minister brought off a superb financial stroke and bought a controlling interest in the Canal from Egypt for four million pounds. "It is just settled, ma'am," he informed her with a flourish. "You have it!"

After that, India became one of her enthusiasms. Bertie was sent on a tour thither and, while he was there, to his utter surprise and considerable annoyance she suddenly had herself proclaimed Empress of India. England did not like the new title and it took all Disraeli's tact to get it through Parliament, but she had her way. In later years, after John Brown's death, it pleased her to have Indian servants to wait on her, and to take a daily lesson in Hindustani.

Meanwhile the great powers of Europe were carving up Africa into colonies for themselves, with

Britain well to the fore. The Liberals, under Gladstone, had no wish to enlarge the Empire. When they were in power the advancing tide either halted or even ebbed. Victoria was scornful of such policies. She was especially furious when General Gordon, sent to evacuate the Sudan, was trapped in Khartoum and killed because the government did not relieve him in time. In her eyes Gladstone was practically Gordon's murderer. Things were better under the Conservatives, even though Disraeli died and gave place to Lord Salisbury. Under them the Union Jack was planted in more and more parts of Africa—east, west, and south.

In 1887 she celebrated her Golden Jubilee, the fiftieth year of her reign. Ten years later followed the Diamond Jubilee, and again the beacon fires blazed from hill to hill. She was very old now, and too lame to walk in any kind of ceremonial procession, but she drove six miles through London streets that were hedged with pink, cheering faces and frenziedly waving flags.

She had come a long way. She had been born in the reign of George III and she had lived to see her great-grandson, the little boy who would one day become George VI. Her reign was an age in itself, the Victorian Age.

What does that phrase stand for in most minds?

Prim manners . . . the kind of false modesty which covered up even furniture legs . . . ugly houses and stuffy rooms . . . bad taste in painting, sculpture, and almost every branch of design . . . hideous factories and shocking slums . . . smug self-satisfaction, hypocritical churchgoing and chapel-going combined with every type of weekday meanness. . . .

All these faults, and more, can be pointed out. The evidence is to be found in the novels of Dickens and in the English towns today. But there is another side to the picture.

The Victorian Age doubled the population—to about thirty-four millions in 1900. Railways transformed the countryside. Not only houses and factories multiplied, but hospitals, schools, and colleges. Britain became greater, richer, and healthier—though not, unfortunately, more beautiful. In science, industry, and the art of government, it was a period of tremendous progress.

However bad its painting and sculpture, at least its literature was first-class. Dickens, Thackeray, the Brontës, George Eliot, Trollope, Meredith, and Hardy were its novelists. Tennyson, Browning, Morris, and Swinburne were its poets. Carlyle, Macaulay, and Ruskin were writing magnificent prose, each in his highly individual way. Now the young reader for the first time had a literature worth reading: it was the age of Charles Kingsley and Lewis Carroll, Rudyard Kipling and Robert Louis Stevenson. Even the theater flowered at the end of the period: in the eighteen-nineties two new playwrights were reviving the long-dead drama, Oscar Wilde and Bernard Shaw. Before that, Gilbert and Sullivan had conquered the world with their light operas. In the realm of more serious music Edward Elgar was already at work.

Other golden ages—Elizabeth's, the Italian Renaissance, ancient Greece and Rome—had their dark and ugly sides, but it is not these which are remembered, once a few centuries have passed. It may well be that the Victorian period will also come to be remembered only for its shining glories.

In the Diamond Jubilee of 1897 those glories reached their climax. As the twentieth century dawned it began to look as though Victoria, like Elizabeth I, had outlived her own epoch.

England by then was fighting a desperate war against the Dutch settlers in South Africa, and suffering disasters such as she had never known. In Europe a new menace was arising—the Kaiser's Germany, so very different from that studious, peace-loving Germany which Albert had admired so loyally. At home society was changing in a manner Victoria found most disagreeable: millionaires were beginning to matter more than marquises, workingmen were organizing into trade unions and political parties, and new authors (so different from the old, respected "men of letters") were poking fun at all the established institutions.

She was eighty-one at the turn of the century. Very old, very tired, but still carrying out her duties, still keeping her journal though now she dictated it because of her failing sight. The end came quickly and gently, on January 22, 1901. The heralds got out their emblazoned uniforms to proclaim Bertie from the battlements of St. James's.

All the pronouns must be changed now. Few men alive could remember the time when they had sung *God Save the King*.

THE YEARS BETWEEN

1901–1926

Victoria's son, Edward VII, was already elderly when he came to the throne, and he died in 1910, to be succeeded by George V, grandfather of her present Majesty. This first quarter of the twentieth century was marked chiefly by World War I, lasting from 1914 to 1918, and the great changes, such as the Russian Revolution and the breakup of the other European empires, which followed it. In this period the British Empire reached its maximum extent, and we see the beginnings of a process unique in history—the peaceful and voluntary transformation of an empire into a free association of states. The change had begun with the Anglo-Saxon dominions, such as Canada, and later the technique was to be applied, with greater difficulty, to such nations as India, Pakistan, and Ceylon. In this period England inevitably lost the position of world leadership she had held in the nineteenth century, having no longer the special advantages or natural resources to maintain her original lead. Apart from military and naval power, however, it was not at all a period of decline. Vigorous progress was made in health, housing, education, and general living conditions. The darker shadows of Victorian England, as shown in the novels of Dickens and elsewhere, retreated before the advance of public opinion.

ELIZABETH II:

HER PRESENT MAJESTY

At a certain moment during the night of February 5 or the early morning of February 6, 1952—no one will ever know the exact time—a princess sitting high up in an African tree became, without realizing it, Queen of England.

A few days earlier, Princess Elizabeth had left home with her husband, the Duke of Edinburgh, on a long overseas tour that her father, King George VI, was not strong enough to make.

After their first round of official engagements, the royal couple had gone to Sagana Lodge in the foothills of Mount Kenya, a little country house, remote and simple, that had been their wedding present from the people of Kenya. A few miles away, in Aberdare Forest, stood the Treetops Hotel, even simpler and more remote—four rooms, resting partly on stilts and partly on the upper branches of a tree, thirty-five feet above the ground and reached only by ladders.

The "hotel" overlooked a water hole, so that guests could watch a steady procession of jungle animals coming to drink. When, as on the night of the royal visit, there was no moon, floodlights were switched on. The Princess spent those hours watching and photographing the big game below. Anyone would have remembered such a night. Unfortunately, for her the pleasure was to be overlaid immediately by the news of the following afternoon.

For during that night George VI died quietly in his sleep at Sandringham. Despite dangerous illnesses and operations, he had been sufficiently fit to carry on his public duties, and even while his daughter strolled through the forest with her motion-picture camera he had spent the afternoon shooting smaller game on his Norfolk estate. But, as the world learned afterward, his life had hung on a thread, and on that February morning his valet entered the King's bedroom to find that he would never wake again.

The news was quickly made public. In East Africa, where it was early afternoon, a journalist received a telephone message that he passed on to the Princess's staff at Sagana Lodge. It was impossible at first to get a call through to London for official confirmation. But when the radio was switched on, the air was full of the news. Only then was the Duke told. He broke it to the Princess—now the Queen. By dusk the next day she was stepping out of her aircraft four thousand miles away in England.

The next morning millions of television viewers watched the Garter King of Arms, wearing the emblazoned herald's tabard, proclaim in sonorous, time-honored phrases that echoed down the centuries:

"Whereas it hath pleased Almighty God to call to His Mercy our late Sovereign Lord King George the Sixth of Blessed and Glorious Memory by whose Decease the Crown is solely and rightfully come to the High and Mighty Princess Elizabeth Alexandra Mary: We, therefore, the Lords Spiritual and Temporal of this Realm, being here assisted with these of His Late Majesty's Privy Council with representatives of the Commonwealth, with other Principal Gentlemen of Quality, with the Lord Mayor, Aldermen and Citizens of London, do now hereby with one voice and Consent of Tongue and Heart publish and proclaim that the High and Mighty Princess Elizabeth Alexandra Mary is now by the Death of our late Sovereign of Happy Memory become Queen Elizabeth the Second, by the Grace of God Queen of this Realm and of all Her other Realms and Territories, Head of the Commonwealth, Defender of the Faith, to whom Her lieges do acknowledge all Faith and constant obedience, with hearty and humble Affection: beseeching God by whom Kings and Queens do reign, to bless the Royal Princess Elizabeth the Second with long and happy Years to reign over us. God save the Queen!"

To all but the elderly, that last cry had an odd ring: it was fifty years since anyone had shouted or sung "God save the *Queen!*" Half a century is a short period measured by dates. But Britain and the world had seen vast changes since the death of Victoria—four kings had come after her. The new Queen was the great-great-granddaughter of the old.

Victoria would have been astounded by the televising of the proclamation of her descendant as Queen, by the aircraft that had so magically brought her home—and by the bush shirt and slacks in which, forty-eight hours earlier, the young Princess had been strolling through the forest. Not all the changes since Victoria's time had been scientific, not all the revolutions political. The whole outlook of women had altered. Even princesses, despite all the traditions surrounding them, shared in the new freedom of their sex.

These changes were well under way when the Princess Elizabeth was born on April 21, 1926. It was fitting that, in the democratic twentieth century, she was born not in a palace but in a house with a number, 17 Bruton Street, Mayfair.

True, it was an impressive house, large, solid, with tall windows between plaster columns. It was the London home of the Earl and Countess of Strathmore, who also owned Macbeth's legendary stronghold at Glamis. It was their daughter, the Lady Elizabeth Bowes-Lyon, who three years before had married the Duke of York, second son of King George V, and who now came home for the birth of her first baby.

The Duchess of York had a warm charm and graciousness that were to become famous the world over when in later years she was Queen and then Queen Mother. She was no foreign princess brought up in a narrow Court atmosphere: though her ancestry was ancient enough, her upbringing had been in touch with everyday things. For a short time she had been to a London day school, and as the youngest but one of ten children she had known the rough-and-tumble of family life.

The Duke was a quiet, shy, conscientious young man who shunned the limelight that beat down so remorselessly on his dashing elder brother, the Prince of Wales. Like Charles I, he had a hesitation in his speech that made public speaking an ordeal, though he learned to conquer the defect with the help of his wife. He loved gardening, country things, and his family. "I was not brought up to be palace-minded," he once remarked wistfully after he was called, most reluctantly, to take the throne.

A few months after the birth of this first child, the Duke and Duchess moved to a large Victorian house nearby at 145 Piccadilly.

Someone who knew the family in those days described the baby as the "golden-haired princess with the brilliant blue gaze."

Her early childhood was as ordinary as her parents could make it. "She was fortunately guarded with discipline and cold sanity at home," wrote Hector Bolitho in his life of George VI. "A young father and mother built up every possible wall of good sense about their child, and she passed through the hazardous state of early girlhood without being spoiled."

Actually, there is seldom much risk of modern

royalty being spoiled in childhood. That belongs to fairy tales. Real princes and princesses are prepared for a hard life of duties and ceremonies, in which they must never make mistakes, never look bored, and—if possible—never be ill. One day's illness may upset innumerable arrangements and disappoint thousands.

Once, it is said, a certain exalted lady was heard to lament: "Oh dear, I'm so tired, my feet ache, and I've got to go round yet another hospital!" "Nonsense!" Queen Mary rebuked her crisply. "You are a member of the British royal family. We are *never* tired—and we all *love* hospitals!"

In those days, children so close in the line of succession to the throne—the young Princess was third—were not sent to school with other boys and girls. They began with governesses and then went on to lessons with brilliant specialist tutors. Their playmates were carefully picked from families close to Palace circles or otherwise acceptable.

In this century British royalty has gradually begun to diminish the stiff and stifling etiquette that surrounded the German-style courts of the Hanoverian sovereigns and Victoria. Even so, with the best will in the world, it is hard for the royal family to enjoy easy and natural contacts with the common man. Wherever they go, it is for the other people a special occasion. "Party manners" are put on. Watchful courtiers and officials see that the conventions are kept. One must not arrive at a function *after* the royal party or leave earlier. One must not speak to royalty unless spoken to, or bring up a new topic of one's own choosing.

Obviously, such rules get broken. Off-duty, as it were, even a king or queen can drop into easy conversation with all kinds of people who serve them—a gamekeeper, say, at Sandringham or Balmoral, or a jockey riding their horses—and on foreign tours they meet countless well-wishers who neither know nor care about the precise rules of protocol observed at Buckingham Palace. Nonetheless, much of royalty's existence passes in a special kind of human isolation.

The Princess was from her earliest years a friendly child, interested in the crowds who always (for some reason she could not at first understand) appeared to be so interested in her. The garden at 145 Piccadilly adjoined the park and she sometimes exchanged a friendly greeting through the railings. Later, she used to enjoy standing at a window high in Buckingham Palace, looking down at the passers-by and wondering about them.

Years afterward, on the eve of her twenty-first birthday, the royal family was visiting the grave of Cecil Rhodes in the wild Matopo Hills. The Princess strolled off by herself.

"There goes Elizabeth, poor lonely girl," King George remarked to one of the Rhodesian ministers. "She will be lonely all her life."

"Shall I go down, sir, and join her?"

"Yes. I should like that."

The Rhodesian picked his way down the hillside.

The Princess heard his footsteps but did not turn her head. "What a wonderful shrine you have here, Mr. Fletcher," she said. In surprise he asked her how she knew who it was behind her. "I saw you with the King," she answered, "and I knew he would send you down to me."

This small incident showed the close understanding that existed between father and daughter.

The Princess's early life was spent at 145 Piccadilly and at Royal Lodge, a house in Windsor Great Park. She spent holidays with her grandparents on both sides of the family.

George V was nearing the end of his twenty-five-year reign. A bluff, bearded, naval figure, he was rather alarming to some people, including his sons. But to the little Princess he was kindly and indulgent, like any other grandfather. He was the last English sovereign molded in the grand nineteenth-century manner, the last to have received, as King-Emperor, the deep salaams of Indian princes under a tropical sun, yet for the Princess ("Lilibet," as she was called in the family) he was seen to grovel good-humoredly on the carpet, looking for a hairclip that had vanished under a sofa.

In the spring of 1929 he was recovering from a grave illness. He asked that Lilibet should be sent to stay with him at the seaside. There was a very real bond between the elderly King and the Princess, strengthened by later visits to the different royal homes and, above all, by the big Christmas gatherings at Sandringham.

Holidays with the Strathmore grandparents were often spent at Glamis, a rugged, rambling Scottish castle like something out of an adventure story, with echoing rooms, long passages, and mysterious stairways to explore.

Here, when Elizabeth was four, her sister, Princess Margaret, was born. The Countess at once called for her car and told her granddaughter to get ready for a drive. They must hurry to the oldest tenant living on the estate and make sure that he and his wife were the first people in the district to know. That was the tradition of good manners in which the Strathmores had been brought up. It might seem an empty formality in an age of telephones and radio, but it meant much to the old couple and their neighbors, who liked to see the traditions carried on. It was a lesson, too, for the Princess, one of the many she was learning all the time.

That night, as the late dusk of a Scottish summer came down on the hills, she was allowed to scramble up to the highest battlements and watch the beacon flame spurt from a summit two miles away. Yonder, her nurse told her, the bagpipes were playing and the people dancing. This was the first royal birth in Scotland since King James had moved south in 1603.

History meant nothing to a four-year-old. What mattered to her was that now she had a sister—a younger sister who, in due course, could be alternately petted and disciplined by her, in the manner of elder sisters the whole world over. "Oh, go away and lose yourself!" she was once overheard to tell Princess Margaret years later in a moment of natural irritation. And doubtless the lively younger girl was often stung to rebellion and retort. Sisters are sisters, however royal.

Miss Marion Crawford, Elizabeth's governess, has recorded how the elder Princess used to cross-examine her about her brother and say:

"I do wish *we* had a brother. . . ."

"Brothers have their drawbacks."

"But how? How, Crawfie? What do you mean, *drawbacks?*"

Nothing the governess could think of would convince her pupil that brothers were not an unmixed blessing in any family.

Miss Crawford took over Elizabeth's education when she was six, but her mother had given her some lessons and she had already learned to read. For French she had a special tutor.

If the modern Elizabeth did not have to pore over so many languages, dead and living, as her Tudor predecessor, she had a great deal more geography to learn, and history—especially Constitutional History.

This is the study of the way in which the British constitution (never set out in one clear document as in the United States and other countries) has slowly evolved from Magna Carta in 1215 to the present day. Over that period the exact powers of the Crown and the two Houses of Parliament, Lords and Commons, have been continually changing. What is to be done in a particular situation has to be decided not by some hard and fast rule but by what happened on previous occasions.

The matter had already become much more complicated in the early twentieth century (and still more so since then) with the creation of completely independent Dominions, such as Canada and Australia already were. These Dominions shared the sovereign on equal terms with Great Britain. They took no orders from the King's ministers in London, but they acknowledged the King as their own sovereign. Though he could not live permanently in Ottawa, Canberra, or any of the other Dominion capitals, King George was, strictly speaking, "King of Canada," "King of Australia," and so on.

In each such country there was a Prime Minister and Cabinet, whose "advice" the King must accept. In each the King appointed a Governor-General to sign documents and perform ceremonial duties on his behalf. It would have been quite possible in theory for the King of England to be at war with a foreign power while as "King of New Zealand" he was at peace.

All this, and much more, the Pincess had to study. Otherwise she might one day make serious mistakes.

It is not true to say that a modern British sovereign has no power and is merely a rubber stamp. True, so long as the government itself observes the laws, there is no need for him to interfere. But if some extraordinary situation were to arise—if, for instance, a party seized control of Parliament by arresting or shutting out its opponents—then the sovereign would certainly have to remember his own responsibilities. He would have to decide whether to sign the laws passed by such a Parliament or to refuse and perhaps act as a rallying point for the people as a whole in their struggle to recover their democratic liberties.

No such thing has ever happened. But there are other, less sensational, ways in which a sovereign has to use personal judgment.

Constitutional History is thus the subject above all others that he must learn, just as an engineer must know mathematics. Needless to say, it is not a nursery subject. It did not trouble the Princess until her father had become King and she herself his "heiress presumptive"—that is, his successor if he had no son.

Her earlier lessons were not so difficult. There were maps to be drawn and colored—there is a pleasant homelike photograph of the two sisters at the round table in their schoolroom, with Princess Margaret stretching over to dip her paintbrush into a glass of water almost under her sister's nose, while the pet dog, a corgi, from whom no intellectual effort is demanded, slumbers blissfully at their feet. And there was poetry to be read aloud and discussed. Early favorites were the more rhythmical, jingling verses of Longfellow, Kipling, and Tennyson—and A. A. Milne's "They're changing guard at Buckingham Palace." The governess tried to interest her elder pupil in more difficult modern poets, but, she afterward recalled, she was apt to be interrupted with the cry: "Oh, do stop! I don't understand a word of it. What *is* the man trying to say?"

There were music and singing lessons, too, popular with both sisters, and a dancing class. Mary and Anne, with similar tastes, had appeared in the elaborate masques of the Stuart Court; Elizabeth and Margaret, during the Second World War, organized Christmas plays at Windsor, taking part as the Prince and Cinderella respectively, or Aladdin and the Princess. In 1944 they did a skit on children's pantomimes, entitled *Old Mother Red Riding Boots*. The sisters also joined with friends and choristers of the Royal Chapel of St. George's at Windsor to form a musical society in which they learned part songs and madrigals.

The young Elizabeth loved riding and swimming —horses were to become a lifelong enthusiasm. Later, as Queen, she was never to look more impressive than when splendidly mounted and in uniform, leading her household troops at the Trooping of the Colour. Nor, of all her public engagements, were any to give her more obvious personal enjoyment than Ascot and other fashionable race meetings at which her own horses were running.

Games had less appeal. Her father, a keen tennis player who had himself competed at Wimbledon, arranged for her to have lessons from the Eton College coach. "Princess Elizabeth has a very good natural eye for the game," reported her instructor, "but I'm afraid she'll never succeed until she forces herself to run after the ball a bit more."

Schoolroom lessons, riding, swimming, country holidays, acting, singing, pets (ranging from dogs to a chameleon), visits to the Zoo, Girl Guiding (the British equivalent of Girl Scout activity), with its opportunity to work and play with other girls—all these made up a full and, on the whole, a happy girlhood. Her parents, however numerous their public duties, always tried to keep time free for the Princesses, usually in the early evening before their bedtime. It became understood that the Duke and Duchess liked to slip away from functions about that time if it could be done without rudeness.

It was less easy after 1936.

Early in that year George V died and was succeeded by the Princesses' Uncle David, the bachelor Prince of Wales, who took the unfamiliar official name of Edward VIII.

As the year passed into autumn, a great constitutional crisis gathered slowly, unknown to the British people, and burst like a sudden thunderstorm.

The new King wished to marry an American. She had been married twice already and was still married, though considering a divorce.

Millions of the King's subjects did not approve of divorce at all. Roman Catholic teaching was definitely against it. The Church of England (of which the King was by law the earthly head) was divided in its views, but few of its members would have cared for a divorce that touched the royal family. The Baptists, Methodists, and others held similar opinions. Divorce might be permissible for private citizens—might, indeed, be the lesser of two evils. But ever since the accession of Victoria, British Royalty had been held up as an example of moral and Christian behavior. A queen, as the first lady in the land, must be someone without a hint of criticism or gossip whom people could look up to.

Then there was the Empire. The great white Dominions were independent of the London government; only their respect for the Crown kept the union. In India and Africa the teeming millions of illiterate peasants understood little of Parliament and the Secretaries of State in Whitehall: they owed allegiance to a person, the King-Emperor. Everything about him must be in keeping with his exalted position. "Everything" included the woman he made his wife and queen.

Even King Edward came to see that the charming Mrs. Simpson, if she got her divorce and were free to marry him, could never win the universal approval of his subjects. He therefore suggested a "morganatic" marriage, such as had been made in foreign royal families. He would marry the woman he loved, but she would not hold the rank of queen.

Constitutional historians looked up their learned volumes, then shook their heads. It had never been done in England. Could it be done now? The Prime Minister, the Archbishop of Canterbury, and most of the other leaders in church and state said "no."

The King thereupon insisted on giving up the throne so that he could be free, as a private person, to marry whom he chose. Not since Richard II had an English king abdicated. The question was: who should succeed him if he went? His brother, the Duke of York, was next in line of succession, but he need not automatically become king. Since the Glorious Revolution of 1688, the Crown had been in the gift of Parliament. He could have stood aside voluntarily or Parliament could have passed him over.

In fact, the Duke did hesitate. His quiet nature shrank from the Crown. Even more, it is said, he thought of the Princess Elizabeth. To accept meant, almost certainly, to accept for her, too—to condemn her to the same cares and duties and make her, as he afterward said, "a poor lonely girl all her life."

But the great need at that moment was to restore the people's shaken respect for the throne. That could not be done if the Crown was given up by one brother, refused by the next, and passed down the line until somebody accepted it. The nation could have split into factions, some favoring one prince, some another. The only safe way was for the eldest to take on the responsibility, putting the country before himself and his family.

Once Edward VIII saw that the nation's leaders were against his plan for a morganatic marriage, he accepted the situation. He made a farewell abdication broadcast, boarded a destroyer, and crossed to France. No longer a king, he was made Duke of Windsor. A few months later he married Mrs. Simpson, who had duly obtained her divorce.

Princess Elizabeth was ten when her father became King George VI. It was all very sudden, alarming in some ways, exciting in others. She was too young to grasp all the consequences.

One sad fact was plain: she must leave "home," at 145 Piccadilly, for the huge rabbit warren of Buckingham Palace, with its miles of corridors and innumerable rooms. It was then that she made a suggestion any child might have made. Could not an underground passage be built, linking the Palace with the house in Piccadilly, "so that we could go home to sleep at night?"

The abdication was only one crisis among many that darkened the nineteen-thirties.

There was the world-wide financial and economic crisis, highlighted in America, where by 1932 the unemployed had risen to twelve millions. In Britain there were three millions, making a somber background to the Princess's sunny childhood. In the Far East there was war between China and Japan. In 1933 Hitler and his Nazi movement seized power in Germany. Mussolini, the Fascist dictator of Italy, conquered the weak and backward African state of Ethiopia. In 1936, a savage civil war erupted in Spain.

The young Princess in Buckingham Palace saw the shadows deepening over the world. In 1938 Hitler seized Austria and threatened Czechoslovakia. Britain and France protested. That September it looked as though war might break out. Shelter trenches against aircraft were hurriedly dug in all the London parks. The Princess, like everyone else, was fitted for a gas mask. Poison gas was the first fear in every mind.

That crisis passed. But in March, 1939, Hitler occupied Czechoslovakia. Poland was next on his list. Britain and France warned him that they would come to her aid. On September 1, the thirteen-year-old Princess, then at Balmoral for the usual summer holiday, learned that Hitler had invaded Poland at dawn. By Sunday morning, September 3, Britain was at war with Germany.

In recent centuries the heads of states had behaved toward one another, even in war, with a certain courtly consideration. Unless by accident, members of royal families had never been in danger of actual physical harm from the other side. The Second World War was different. The Princess and her family shared the same dangers as everyone else in Britain, and rather more than the average.

Royal blood was no protection now. If anything, it made one a target. Soon the British were welcoming the fugitive Queen of the Netherlands, as, her country overrun, she made her way to safety in Canada. The rugged old King of Norway brought tales of having to lie in a ditch while questing German aircraft sprayed the road with machine guns. The Kings of Greece and Yugoslavia were also in exile. The Kings of Denmark and Belgium were Hitler's prisoners.

In the blackest year, 1940, when Britain feared invasion, thousands of children were sent to Canada or the United States. If the Princesses had been anyone else's daughters, they might have gone. But again George VI put his country before his family. If they had been sent across the Atlantic, if would have been a sign that even the King had lost confidence. It would have spread doubt and fear everywhere.

Princess Elizabeth and her sister spent the war years at Windsor, outside London—like hundreds of thousands of other evacuees who were distributed through the country areas to escape the bombs and, later, the rockets that destroyed so much of London and the big cities.

Buckingham Palace was among the slightly damaged buildings. The old home in Piccadilly was blown to pieces.

In October, 1940, the fourteen-year-old Princess made her first radio broadcast, to the children of the Empire. "I can truthfully say to you all," she said, "that we children at home are full of cheerfulness and courage. We are trying to do all we can to help our gallant soldiers, sailors, and airmen, and we are trying, too, to bear our share of the danger and sadness of war. We know, every one of us, that in the end all will be well."

For the first half of the war Princess Elizabeth's primary duty was that of every other boy and girl: to continue her education and fit herself for the future. On her sixteenth birthday, however, she had to register her name for National Service, though young people were not actually called into the armed forces or to other work until they were eighteen.

During the two years between, the Princess began to make public appearances and by degrees to get used to all kinds of ceremonies and functions. Her eighteenth birthday meant even more to her than to other girls, for at that point she became old enough to serve as one of the Counsellors of State exercising the powers of the King if he were absent abroad. She served in this role when her father visited the war fronts in France and the Mediterranean. And from this date onward, if the King had died, she would have become Queen with full powers and without any regency to take over the responsibility.

She was not so concerned with this vague possibility as with the definite fact that she was now eighteen and that girls of her age were doing useful, often dangerous, work in the various services.

"Look what Mary's doing," she reminded her father. Lady Mary Cambridge, her cousin, was nursing in the bomb-devastated East End of London. "And I am just stuck down here doing nothing."

The King finally allowed her to join the Auxiliary Territorial Service, later the Women's Royal Army Corps. Though not mechanically minded, she went into the transport section, took the usual course in the driving and maintenance of vehicles, and was commissioned as an ordinary officer of junior rank. From babyhood she had always been fascinated by uniforms and drill. The few months during which she was fully and truly a working Army officer were a happy interlude in her life.

That summer, 1945, saw the surrender of Germany and then, just after the dropping of the first atomic bombs on Japan, the end also of the war in the Far East. Between those two events Britain held a General Election that produced a surprise defeat for Winston Churchill and the first Parliament with a clear (in fact, overwhelming) Labor majority. So, for the first time in history, the British sovereign had Socialist ministers with complete political power. But British Socialists (unlike many in Europe) had never on the whole favored a republic, and the new government made no difference whatever to the position of the royal family.

When the victory cheering had died away and the bonfires were burned to cold gray ashes, Britain's future also looked somewhat gray and cold.

The country had been blasted and bombed by the enemy, so that great tracts of her cities, her docks and factories, lay in ruins. Her people were tired. She had been forced to sell much of her property abroad, such as her investments in North and South America, to pay for the six years of costly war. She was now short of money to pay for reconstruction and for imports of food and raw materials.

Her Empire was restless. India was demanding independence without further delay; this was granted, with good will as far as the British were concerned but with much discord and bloodshed between the Hindu and Moslem sections of the population, so that not one independent state but two, India and Pakistan, had to be created. Never now would the Princess inherit Victoria's proud title of Queen-Empress.

There was violence, too, when Palestine broke away—part to form the Jewish state of Israel, part to enlarge the neighboring Arab Kingdom of Jordan. Malaya, freed from Japanese occupation, became at once the scene of a guerrilla jungle warfare against the British. There were special difficulties in Africa. The peoples of the eastern and western colonies were demanding more and more rights and, to a certain degree, receiving them from a friendly government in London. The British of all parties were willing enough to grant the Africans eventual independence; it was a question of "how soon?" How soon, that is, would these countries have leaders sufficiently trained and democratic systems firmly enough established to stand on their own feet?

In South Africa, again, an entirely different policy was being followed toward the non-white majority of the inhabitants. South Africa was still at that time a Dominion of the British Empire. Her government spoke, nominally, in the King's name. But the words were quite different from those of the King's government in Britain (which was responsible for the territories of West and East Africa) because that one had been elected by the citizens of the United Kingdom, while the South African government represented only a white minority, mainly Afrikaners of Dutch ancestry.

To all these problems of home and Empire were added those of Europe and elsewhere. Victory had brought immediate disunity to the victors. The world was dividing, more and more definitely, into two bitter and suspicious halves, the one dominated by the United States, the other by the Soviet Union, with the extra complication of a Communist China soon to come.

These were not problems to be solved quickly. The Princess could not fail to realize that many of them would last into the next reign, however far away that might be. On her twenty-first birthday, during the royal family's tour of South Africa in

1947, she broadcast a memorable speech from Cape Town and ended:

"I can make my solemn act of dedication with a whole Empire listening. I should like to make that dedication now. It is very simple. I declare before you all that my whole life, whether it be long or short, shall be devoted to your service and the service of the great imperial family to which we all belong, but I shall not have the strength to carry out this resolution alone unless you join in it with me, as I now invite you to do. I know that your support will be unfailingly given. God help me to make good my vow and God bless all of you who are willing to share it."

A few months later her engagement was announced.

As the abdication of Edward VIII had so recently shown, the choice of royal husbands and wives was still a matter of considerable public importance. But at least the age had passed when princesses had to be sacrificed, for the sake of an alliance, to foreigners they disliked or had never seen. The King's daughter could not marry just anyone, but few people really can; most of us choose our partner from the same social and religious group as our own. The social group was smaller for a princess, but within it she was free to choose according to her natural feelings.

Prince Philip of Greece was then twenty-six. He had been born on the island of Corfu in 1921, the son of Prince Andrew of Greece and nephew of the

British admiral, Earl Mountbatten. Like the Princess, he was a descendant of Queen Victoria. He had been educated in France, Germany, and Scotland; after that, at eighteen, he had entered the Royal Naval College at Dartmouth, where he had won the King's Dirk as the best cadet of his term. Later, on the battleship *Valiant,* he had fought in the Mediterranean battle of Cape Matapan, and witnessed the official Japanese surrender in the Far East.

The Prince's character had thus been formed mainly outside the restricted circles of royal courts. For all his exalted ancestry, he commanded neither great wealth nor influence: the Greek royal family had been in exile for most of his boyhood and did not count for much. Nor did he stand very near the Greek throne, though he had his place in the line of succession to it. This he formally gave up when he became a naturalized British subject before his marriage.

Essentially, in appearance, outlook, and upbringing, the Prince was as British as anyone at Windsor. He loved his chosen career in the Royal Navy. His taste was for vigorous outdoor recreations, especially polo and the racing of small sailing boats. He liked informality and was quick to see through humbug, not least the deceptive sort of show often mounted to impress royal visitors. He had a quiet, throwaway kind of humor. If he had never had time or perhaps inclination to develop the deeper intellectual interests, he brought an alert mind, sharpened by naval training, to those scientific and technical subjects, increasingly vital in the new world, that had not previously tended to come the way of royalty.

The Princess had seen him frequently in childhood, but then a difference of five years had been too wide for real friendship. The gap narrowed during the war, as she grew up. The Prince spent several periods of leave with the royal family. When he went on active service the couple corresponded regularly. Though their engagement was not announced until 1947, it is probable that they settled the question privately between themselves the previous summer, during a holiday at Balmoral.

They were married on November 20, 1947, in Westminster Abbey, with a blend of ancient pageantry and modern publicity. The Prince, who had become a British citizen in the previous February and was legally Lieutenant Mountbatten, was made Duke of Edinburgh on the eve of the wedding. Not until ten years later was he created a Prince of the Realm and so entitled once more to be called "Prince" Philip.

There is a pleasant anecdote about the wedding preparations. The Princess wanted to include in the service a particular descant she and her sister had been accustomed to sing as they drove home from a day on the Scottish hills. She therefore telephoned the Precentor, who was in charge of the music at the Abbey, and asked if it could be done. "Certainly, Your Royal Highness," came the answer. "Where is this particular setting published?" "I don't think it *is* published. Can you take it down if I hum it to you?" Paper and pencil were hurriedly seized, the tune was duly hummed over the wire, but somehow it refused to be transferred to the paper. Rather flustered, the Precentor called the organist to the telephone. The humming was obligingly repeated, but it still defied the efforts of both musicians to transcribe it. "May we come round to the Palace?" they suggested, and in a very short time, with the help of a piano and Princess Margaret, the elusive notes were pinned down on paper.

The next four years were full ones. For the first time Princess Elizabeth had a home of her own, Clarence House, furnished according to her ideas.

There were more and more public duties. There was a trip to Paris, her first on foreign soil, and four to Malta, where the Duke was stationed for two years with the Navy. From there they visited the Pope and the King of Greece.

A tour of Canada, over the Rockies to the Pacific, showed them cowboy rodeos, American Indians, winter sports, and the revived pastime of square dancing, which the Princess's example helped to make fashionable in Britain. There was an all-too-brief visit to the American President at Washington. Finally, there there was the ill-fated tour planned for East Africa, Ceylon, Australia, and New Zealand, cut short almost before it had begun.

Soon, too, there was a family to think of: Prince Charles born on November 14, 1948, Princess Anne on August 15, 1950. Following her parents' example, the Princess was determined that the children should not suffer because of the life she was already forced to lead.

When she became Queen, she altered the time of her regular weekly talk with the Prime Minister—the time favored by her father clashed with the hour of play, between tea and bed, that she tried to reserve for her children. She would have been the first to agree with the Dean of Westminster when he preached in the Abbey, a few days after her accession: "The Queen, God bless her, is young, fresh, and full of vitality. Let us give her a chance of being not only a queen but a woman with a home to enjoy and a mother with children for whom to care."

The pressure of duties upon a British sovereign is hard for an outsider to imagine.

There are, of course, countless occasions that are purely social. Hospital-openings, parades, charity performances, national sporting events, and many similar affairs can be shared with other members of the royal family, but there are countless functions the Queen must attend herself. The state visit of a foreign ruler is one example. The guest must be welcomed by the Queen at Victoria Station and driven in procession to Buckingham Palace, where later a banquet is given in his honor, at which the Queen proposes his health. Another day the visiting ruler entertains the Queen to a return banquet at his country's London embassy, and all the involved ceremonial is repeated in reverse. Then, within a year or two, the Queen must pay a similar state visit to the country in question, following out the same unalterable pattern of banquets, luncheons, wreath-laying at national shrines, and so on.

This, any ordinary person might feel, could be interesting and even enjoyable occasionally. But in the first fourteen years of her reign Queen Elizabeth paid state visits of this type to Norway, Sweden, Portugal, France, Denmark, Holland, Italy, Germany, Belgium, and thirteen other countries, as well as visiting thirty more without the full ceremonial, as when she twice entered the United States from Canada. In all those travels, however, she did not once set foot in any of the Communist territories now covering so much of the world, for this would have caused much diplomatic difficulty, though Prince Philip has made no secret of his own inclination for a Russian visit if such difficulties could be overcome.

State visits and Commonwealth tours form only a fraction of the Queen's work. Almost every day, when she is at Buckingham Palace, there are people to be received. A newly appointed foreign ambassador may arrive, in full regalia and driven in the carriage thoughtfully provided, to present his credentials. A resigning minister may come to surrender his seals of office, or, if just promoted, to "kiss hands on his appointment," and other callers may be honored with "an audience of the Queen" or even stay for lunch. Sometimes there is a morning investiture, when the Queen bestows orders and medals, or an afternoon garden party in the shady grounds that lie, unexpectedly spacious, behind the long façade of Buckingham Palace.

Most of this goes on, unaltered, whoever occupies

the throne. Officials dislike changes. So—in royal matters—do many of the public. But they *are* made. The young Queen soon abolished the much criticized ritual of "presentation," when young girls, or "debutantes," were ceremonially introduced, made their painfully rehearsed curtsies to the Queen, and were smoothly ushered from the Court that few were ever likely to set foot in again. By contrast, the Queen and Prince Philip instituted small, informal lunch parties, inviting a handful of guests, each distinguished is some field, scientific or artistic, commercial or athletic, who would be interesting to talk to but who would not normally be met in Palace circles.

It would take pages to indicate the full variety of the Queen's working routine, day by day and month by month. The weekly conversations with her Prime Minister have been mentioned. There are other meetings with him before special occasions or at times of crisis. At the state opening of Parliament she has to deliver "the Queen's Speech," which is actually prepared by the government of the day and represents their views, not necessarily her own: this speech, nonetheless, she must discuss with the Prime Minister. And the Chancellor of the Exchequer, before presenting his Budget to Parliament—his survey of the nation's financial affairs and his program for taxation—always visits the Queen and gives her a preview of what he intends.

Is all this a waste of her time and theirs, it may be asked, seeing that under the democratic system she has no power to block the will of Parliament or the legal actions of her ministers?

The truth is not so simple as it looks. "Power" and "influence" are not always quite the same thing. Parents and other experienced people have no "power" they can enforce on children once they have grown up, but if those children have come to respect their parents' opinions they do not lose all "influence" just because the children are over twenty-one. Similarly, a British sovereign, even while still young in years, gathers an inside knowledge of men and affairs—not least, foreign affairs—that many a politician envies. Politicians come and go, in and out of office. The Queen goes on without interruption. Thus, in her first few years, she had Churchill as Prime Minister, then Sir Anthony Eden, Mr. Harold Macmillan, Sir Alec Douglas-Home, and the Labor leader, Mr. Harold Wilson. To them, or to their foreign ministers, she could talk of many things she had learned in her travels, and often of key figures abroad whom she had known at first hand but whom the newly appointed minister had still to meet and assess. The Queen can never tell her ministers *what* to do, but there are moments when, because of all the contacts she has had in the past, she can give them a useful idea of the people with whom they are dealing.

The famous royal memory is not just a flair for recognizing an old soldier in the ranks or saying the right word to the right person. It is the gift of storing information and gathering political wisdom, which can be made available to (but never forced upon) the ever-changing group of politicians who form the government of the day.

As with conversations, so with innumerable papers the Queen has to sign. Is it a waste of time? Might she not just as well scrawl a swift signature upon them, unread—or even use a rubber stamp? Neither the Queen nor her father nor her grandfather has ever thought so. Even in a modern democracy the sovereign is allowed a tactful query or suggestion, and once more the royal memory may come into play, recalling what happened on some previous occasion that everyone else has forgotten.

A constitutional sovereign may not be able to say "no" to his ministers, but that does not mean he is allowed to say nothing at all.

A ruling queen must perform all the political functions of a king, but, just because she remains a woman, she has to do more besides.

A king usually has a wife, a queen consort who is free from all political responsibilities and can give up her energies, like the wives of other public figures, to acting as hostess and otherwise lightening the social burden for her husband.

Where the roles of the sexes are reversed, it is not possible just to switch over all the duties. Though helping and supporting the Queen in innumerable ways, Prince Philip could scarcely take over the part of a hostess. He had his own problems of adjustment to the difficult position of a prince consort. He knew that he must never interfere in political matters by trying to influence the Queen: the British people, always jealous of Albert's domination of Victoria, would never allow that situation to arise again. Yet the Prince had far too much character and ability to sink completely into the background, like Queen Anne's long-forgotten husband. Prince Philip, once he had had to renounce his career in the Navy, found his own solution. He carved out his own niche in public life, identifying himself actively with all kinds of progressive movements—scientific and technological education, better industrial management, and the encouragement of initiative among young people working for his "Duke of Edinburgh's Award."

So, when they were together in public, the Prince had always to take second place to the Queen. But in private he was, like most husbands, very much the head of the family, and the Queen, given the rare pleasure of a day free from official duties, could relax thankfully into the role of wife and mother.

On February 19, 1960, Elizabeth gave birth to a son, Prince Andrew, the first child born to a reigning British sovereign for a century. Four years later, on March 3, 1964, came Prince Edward.

By then, Prince Charles was fifteen and his only sister thirteen, and one question that had been asked by many was already answered: would the royal children, in the mid-twentieth century, be subjected to the old narrow Court education by tutors and governesses or would they be sent to school to mix freely with people of their own age? School was decided upon. And for the Prince it was not Eton, the school most favored by the aristocracy and upper classes, but his father's old school in Scotland, Gordonstoun, where the emphasis was perhaps rather more on character-building and adventurous physical pursuits (sailing and mountain rescue and fire-fighting) than on scholarship, conventional games, and sophistication. Toward the end of his time at Gordonstoun, Prince Charles (by now Prince of Wales) went out to spend a term or two on educational exchange at Geelong Grammar School in Australia. In deciding all this for the training of the future King Charles III of England it is obvious that Prince Philip's views carried a good deal of weight.

When Queen Elizabeth came to the throne the Conservatives had just regained power in Britain under the popular but aging wartime leader, Winston Churchill. Later that year, the Republicans won the Presidency of the United States, where another great wartime leader, General Eisenhower, was to hold office for the next eight years. In Russia the dictator Stalin died and there seemed some hope of easier relations between East and West.

In those first years the young Queen had the advantage of working with a Prime Minister whose memory of public affairs stretched back, almost unbelievably, to the reign of her great-great-grandmother, and who moreover had been a trusted and intimate friend of her father during the Second World War. By 1955 Churchill was eighty-one and too infirm to carry on. He "advised" the Queen (for so runs the polite phrasing) to send for Sir Anthony Eden as his successor. In theory the Queen still chooses her ministers. In practice she must appoint the man with a majority in Parliament.

Eden was unfortunate. His own health was failing and he immediately ran into trouble abroad: the Suez Canal "incident" of 1956, when British and French forces, simultaneously with the Israelis, attacked Egypt and tried to regain control of the waterway. British public opinion was fiercely divided by what had been a discreditable muddle, however well meant. But it was Eden's health, even more than the outcry, that drove him into retirement. He was followed by two more Conservative leaders, the urbane and elegant Harold Macmillan and then, as a brief stopgap, Sir Alec Douglas-Home, who renounced an ancient earldom so that he could lead the government in the House of Commons. Then the General Election brought the Labor Party to power again, and their leader, Harold Wilson, became the Queen's fifth Prime Minister in twelve years.

And, it must be remembered, she had many other Prime Ministers: the men heading her governments in the various Dominions that still acknowledged her as their Queen. But a complete change was coming over the face of the Commonwealth. The Empire of her predecessors was already a thing of the past.

It had become the custom that, every few years, there should be an informal conference of Dominion Prime Ministers in London. In 1955 they still formed a small group, nearly all sharing the same British blood, background, and general outlook. Less than ten years later the group had grown: one after another, the old imperial possessions had won their independence and, with it, the right to send a representative. The enlarged conference table was ringed with new faces from Africa, Asia, and the West Indies. South Africa, no longer at home in such company, threw off her allegiance to the Queen and became a republic. Many of the new states, for other reasons, declared themselves republics but remained inside the group. Elizabeth II ceased to be their Queen but was acknowledged in a special role as head of the Commonwealth. These new developments brought new problems, as when, in 1965, the white minority in Rhodesia declared its independence and, while still emphasizing its devotion to the Queen, defied the authority of her ministers in London.

It was then eighteen years since, as a young princess, she had publicly dedicated her life to "the service of our great imperial family." How would she be able to fulfill that promise in the further years ahead? And—to consider quite another problem of a dizzily changing world—where would she stand if Britain, having entered the Common Market, gradually merged her own independence into a tightly knit European community?

Whatever the future for Queen Elizabeth II in the second half of her life, it could hardly lack incident and interest.

AUTHOR'S NOTE

It is impossible to list all the historical works, general and special, which have been consulted during the writing of this book, but the author is particularly indebted to the following among the more recent biographers: R. W. A. O. Onslow (*Empress Maud,* 1939); H. F. M. Prescott (*Spanish Tudor,* 1940) and B. M. I. White (*Mary Tudor,* 1935); J. E. Neale (*Queen Elizabeth,* 1934) and Milton Waldman (*Elizabeth,* 1933); G. M. V. Long (*The Third Mary Stuart,* 1933); Neville Connell (*Anne, The Last Stuart Monarch,* 1937) and M. R. Hopkinson (*Anne of England,* 1934); E. F. Benson (*Queen Victoria,* 1935), Dr. Edith Sitwell (*Victoria of England,* 1936), and Lytton Strachey (*Queen Victoria,* 1921); Marion Crawford (*The Little Princesses,* 1950) and Frances Towers (*The Two Princesses,* 1941).